COUNTRY LIVING

Living with
FOLK ART

Danna and
Larrey—
Thanks for inviting
Kate to Share.
Ben & Diane

COUNTRY LIVING

Living with
FOLK ART

Text by Rebecca Sawyer-Fay

HEARST BOOKS
New York

Library of Congress Cataloging-in-Publication Data
Country living, living with folk art / by the editors of Country Living
magazine.—1st ed.
    p. cm.
    1. Ethnic art in interior decoration. 2. Interior decoration—
United States. I. Country living (New York, N.Y.) II. Title: Living
with folk art.
NK2115.5E84C68   1994
747'.9—dc20   94-6366
                                                      CIP

ISBN 0-688-11666-3 (hc), 1-58816-008-4 (pb)

Printed in Singapore
First Paperback Edition 2001
1 2 3 4 5 6 7 8 9 10

Produced by Smallwood & Stewart, Inc., New York City
Edited by Rachel Carley
Design by Julio Vega

Front cover photograph by Keith Scott Morton
Back cover photographs (top left and to right) by Al Teufen,
(bottom left) Keith Scott Morton, and (bottom right) Lynn Karlin.

www.countryliving.com

*A whitewashed birdhouse by contemporary
artist Dean Johnson is set off by a Mennonite crib quilt
(page 1). A railroad sign from Maine (page 2)
conveys a warm welcome. An 1880s Bucks County,
Pennsylvania, home (right) features striking portraits and
a grain-painted Pennsylvania-German settle.
German sheep figures are displayed on a tobacco sorter with
graduated shelves (page 6). A 19th-century embroidery,
Early American schoolchildren's drawings, and
miniature chairs are among the eye-catching objects in a
Manhattan apartment (page 8). Shells make an
unusual heart-shaped picture frame (page 10). Dating
from the late-Victorian era, a Tramp Art clock (page 152)
still works. Mexican-American game boards and
an 1840s acorn-finial bed distinguish a Santa Fe home
(page 156). Three painted-wood dogs and one real
one enjoy a hill-top romp (page 160).*

CONTENTS

FOREWORD

I remember with great joy the day my father finished crafting a miniature re-creation of a famous fishing shack in Rockport, Massachusetts. The fishing shack held much character from years of weathering, and it had piqued my father's interest for some time. Our living room was transformed when that tiny fishing shack — complete with wharf and pilings — was placed atop the fireplace mantel. With time, the shack has made its way to *my* living room mantel, where it is displayed with great pride and a fond affection for the memories it brings. And never mind the new paint, the sofa, or the view — the first thing that guests notice is my father's work of art! Invariably, their eyes light up as mine did that very first day. It is precisely with this spirit in mind that we at *Country Living* created a book dedicated entirely to folk art.

This project has generated much excitement. I recently had lunch with Gerard Wertkin, Director of The Museum of American Folk Art in New York City, and he was delighted to hear about the creation of this book, explaining, "By its very nature, folk art draws from the cultures of all Americans. The field has always celebrated the work of women, as well as African-Americans and other ethnic groups in a way that encourages a coming together rather than a seperation. It is this quality that has made folk art inclusive and accessible."

With modernity comes a constant need to assess what one keeps and what one discards. The origins of folk art, however, are far removed from the present day mania of what is fashionable and what is not. Folk art was a layman's art. Created by artisans with no formal training, folk art carries with it a unique tradition in which household necessities are empowered with an endless creative energy.

Living with Folk Art integrates this spirit of folk art into our individual sense of style, weaving the necessary with the pleasurable, blending the past with the present. Within these pages, decorative qualities such as shape, color, humor, and whimsy bring a new lease on life to every room in the home. Colorful hooked rugs embellish a wall, a collection of woven baskets adds layers of texture and shading to a room, and a quilt's patchwork of vivacious colors gives character to a bedroom. And, like my father's tiny fishing shack, the art within these pages is appreciative of the gracious genius of its artisans, most of them unnamed, who use the richness of their lives as inspiration.

Before Gerard Wertkin and I wrapped up our leisurely lunch, he noted, "At The Museum of American Folk Art, we find folk art is appreciated as never before. Serious scholarship is bringing new and fresh insights to its study, while Americans in increasing numbers are drawn to its appealing qualities." We welcome this opportunity to celebrate folk art in the American hearth and home.

Rachel Newman
Founding Editor
Country Living

INTRODUCTION

As we peruse the beautifully decorated rooms in this book and admire how examples of American folk art fit naturally into our homes today, it is easy to forget how relatively short the history of folk art collecting is in this country. Among the first to appreciate the aesthetics of folk art—the rough paint of a well-used decoy, the flat perspective of a child's portrait, the weathered patina of an antique weather vane—were modern and abstract artists. In the early 20th-century, these foresighted individuals, such as Marsden Hartley, Yasuo Kuniyoshi, William Zorach, Charles Sheeler, and Elie Nadelman, saw a distinct relationship between the abstract qualities of folk sculpture and painting and their own art, and often used the earlier works as inspiration.

Many of the great folk art collections were assembled shortly thereafter, during the 1930s and 1940s, by people who began simply by buying objects and paintings as decoration suitable for their old houses or to complement their Early American furniture. The material was plentiful, inexpensive, and sometimes rescued directly from the trash bin. Jean Lipman, one of the earliest and most prolific writers and collectors in the field, likes to tell the story of how she and her husband, Howard, paid 50 cents for a painting called "Winter Sunday in Norway, Maine," which has since been reproduced, published, and exhibited many times and was even used on a U.S. postage stamp.

Clearly, good folk art is no longer inexpensive, nor is it found in great quantities. Therefore, as in any field, it is important to be an informed consumer. One of the consequences of the current interest in folk art and country decorating is the proliferation of objects made today to appeal to new collectors, many of whom are confused about the difference between traditional folk art, craft, and contemporary imitations.

There are true folk artists working today. Most of these self-taught men and women live in isolated communities and their artwork tends to be strong and idiosyncratic, and bears little resemblance to traditional 18th- and 19th-century antiques. There are also fine artists and craftspeople who are consciously creating objects inspired—not unlike the work of those very first artist/collectors—by the folk art of yesterday. Pieces by some of these artists are featured in this volume. However, there are also people who simply seek to capitalize on the trend; they neglect to sign and date their work and hope to fool the untrained eye into buying something new in the hopes that it is old, or into believing that it is true folk art.

Only experience can train your eye. One of the best ways to learn more about folk art is to visit museums. A number of the early collections are now available to the public, housed in museums and other institutions where they form the core of extensive holdings in the folk art field. The Lipmans' first collection, for example, was sold to the New York State Historical Association in Cooperstown, New York; much of their their second assemblage now resides at the Museum of American Folk Art in New York City. The Abby Aldrich Rockefeller Folk Art Center in Williamsburg, Virginia, houses a collection first exhibited at the Museum of Modern Art in New York City in 1932. To properly display her decoys, paintings, quilts, trade signs, and other objects, another collector, Electra Havemayer Webb, moved historic buildings onto her property in Burlington, Vermont, to form the Shelburne Museum. These institutions often sponsor traveling exhibitions that enable people in other parts of the country to view their collections. A number of other regional institutions, such as the Milwaukee Museum of Art and the Museum of International Folk Art in Santa Fe, have started their own collecting programs.

Perhaps the most overlooked sources for collections and information about folk art are local museums, historical societies, and libraries. Much—if not most—folk art was produced in rural areas, and it is common to find portraits, landscapes, painted furniture, quilts, needlework, trade signs, and other artifacts in the small house museums and history collections located in towns and villages across the country. Libraries are also often repositories of objects and documents of local historical significance and can be gold mines for researching the genealogical or historical background of a work.

Books such as *Living with Folk Art* can also help increase your understanding of the subject. Looking at the homes reproduced on these pages allows you to see fine pieces in the most flattering settings, displayed to best advantage. Reading the text will provide a good introduction to this extensive field. Other books, noted in the selected bibliography, will provide in-depth information and visual references on the specific areas of folk art that interest you. And the more you look, the more you will be able to see for yourself the differences between art and artifact, and between what is authentic folk art and what is merely "folky."

Elizabeth V. Warren
Consulting Curator
Museum of American Folk Art, New York

PART ONE

ORIGINS OF FOLK ART

Every time we admire a sampler embellished with delicate stitches, a patch-work quilt still loved after generations of use, or a hand-woven Navajo Chief's blanket, we have America's rich mix of cultures to thank. Owing its earliest folk art traditions to native groups, North America is also a continent of immigrants, enriched by the heritages of peoples from virtually every corner of the world. While settlers often arrived in the New World with few tangible possessions, they came with skilled hands and a wealth of artistic traditions.

Unpretentious, inventive, and free-spirited, folk art of all peoples and cultures encompass-

es purely decorative works of art, such as paintings, as well as utilitarian objects. The term is loosely defined as the creative expression of artisans without formal train-ing; taken as a whole, that expression can represent the collective soul of a nation, province, ethnic group, or community. Distinctive needlework and weaving pat-terns, carving techniques, and other craft customs are the means by which cultural identities are handed down from generation to generation.

Perhaps most significant, folk art has proved an outlet for an impulse to create that tran-scends time, geography, and gender. During frigid winters centuries ago, Swedish men spent long hours carving a sin-gle chair. Farther east, Russian women fashioned ornaments for the *krasni ugol,* or "beautiful corner," always located in the right-hand corner of the kitchen. In Italy and France, potters crafted tiles in the sunny colors of the Mediterranean. Organic by nature, the count-less folk art traditions of these and other peoples evolved slow-ly but surely, the product of religious beliefs, patriotic fervor, environment, and everyday needs. To our good fortune, the customs continued in this country. Confronted by new challenges and materials, immi-grants adapted to the unfamiliar land and went right on creating, giving us new forms of folk art and untold treasures waiting to be explored.

Stylized dragon heads (above) top the roof gables at Little Norway, a restored 19th-century Norwegian homestead in Blue Mounds, Wisconsin. According to Scandinavian legend, the heads kept evil spirits at bay. Inside the main cabin of the homestead (opposite), the whole family slept in a master bed like this one, the younger children in the lower drawers. The three-legged chair, called a bandestol, was originally designed for stability on an earthen floor.

EUROPE

Lack of factory-made materials and isolation from urban centers are largely responsible for the vitality and originality so evident in European folk art. Faced with limited resources, Old World artisans were self-sufficient by both inclination and necessity, often relying on handmade tools and homemade paints and dyes. The telltale marks left by hand-wrought chisels, and the natural colors derived from berries and bark also contributed a human touch and warmth to furniture, textiles, and other crafts that the assembly line could never match.

Throughout Europe, each country, and in some cases specific villages, developed signature techniques and motifs depending in large part on climate and available materials. In 18th-century Scotland, for instance, country folk were more likely to be found weaving than carving, since wool was plentiful and wood in short supply. (The tradition continued in America, where Scottish weavers gained wide renown for their beautiful coverlets.)

By contrast, in lands across the North Sea, where forests once seemed inexhaustible, whittling filled endless hours on winter days when it was too cold to venture outdoors. Swedes carved intricate darning

tools and kitchen utensils, particularly spoons, which they presented to loved ones. Similarly, in the Bavarian and Ötztal Alps, Tyrolean folk artists gained a reputation for finely crafted furnishings, including beds, chairs, cupboards, and dower chests. Polish woodworkers, in turn, honed the art of chip carving, done with an ax or hatchet, and notch carving, distinguished by V-shaped knife cuts.

Religion also played a major role in shaping folk art traditions. For instance, some German folk sculpture appeared only on holy days. On Palm Sunday, half-size Christ figures called *Palmesel* made their way through village streets, seated on carved wooden "donkeys" fastened to wheels. At Christmastime, diminutive holy families came alive in countless crèche scenes across the land. Interpreted by the Moravians and other Protestant sects, these biblical tableaux took the form of the *Putz*, an elaborate miniature re-creation of an entire village.

A late-19th-century Swedish sewing box (left) features traditional Scandinavian painted decoration, while Norwegian embroidery (above) shows characteristically fine stitching. As in much European needlework, red is the dominant color, symbolizing love, passion, and life itself.

Another legacy of Germanic cultures was the art of hand-lettered fraktur. Developed in response to European laws requiring certificates of birth, baptism, marriage, and death, fraktur decoration frequently graced the pages of hymnals, Bibles, and prayer books, becoming the folk art equivalent of medieval illuminated manuscripts. Often, fraktur, perfected in America by the Pennsylvania Germans, was the work of professional calligraphers who scribed documents for people who couldn't write.

In Scandinavia and Russia, the influence of

religion on folk art is perhaps best expressed by church buildings, whose carved gables, bargeboards, and other trim represent the zenith of the artists' handwork. Textiles, too, were frequently woven with sacred meaning as well as with yarn. Inside the chimneyless cottages of rural Scandinavia, for example, gay woven hangings and embroidered banners were practical. Besides covering smoke-darkened walls, they also signaled the arrival of feast days and weddings.

Sometimes the symbolism of Christianity and paganism melded together, resulting in folk art

Intricate hand-forged metalwork embellishes the embroidered sleeve of a Norwegian costume (above left). Colorful Easter eggs (above right) are a Ukrainian tradition. To decorate these pysanky, artisans paint the uncooked white egg with beeswax, then dip it into dye baths; the unwaxed areas absorb the color.

rooted in ancient beliefs but used to celebrate the highest holy days. The exquisitely decorated Easter eggs of Ukraine, Poland, and other Slavic nations, for example, are a primitive symbol of renewed life transformed into an emblem of Christ's resurrection.

In remote areas where Calvinism and other sobering doctrines were slowest to take hold, high spirits mark the creative output of Europe's folk artists. A noteworthy example is the Norwegian art of rosemaling, or rose painting, originating in the rich ornamental heritage of the ninth-century Vikings. Three basic brushstrokes—a C, an S, and a circle—were used to create robust, colorful designs on furniture and walls. One prominent rosemaling motif, the acanthus leaf, traveled home to Norway with the Vikings after an assault on Rome, where the invaders saw it used to decorate Corinthian columns. Eventually, the acanthus and other plant motifs completely replaced the serpents and mythological creatures once central to Norwegian design.

Some of Scandinavia's most renowned folk painters were among the many Norwegians who

The geometric designs carved into a 19th-century Norwegian monk's chair (opposite) mimic the embroidered motifs on the curtains. The hand-loomed fabric seat is original. Painted on the side of a trunk, a lady on horseback (above) is complemented by a gentleman on the other side. This is a contemporary example of the traditional Norwegian art of rosemaling.

emigrated to America to take advantage of the Homestead Act of 1862. Many hailed from the remote provinces of Telemark and Hallingdal, where the art of rosemaling had attained its greatest popularity. Once settled in Wisconsin, Illinois, Iowa, and Minnesota, these accomplished craftspeople continued their work and introduced a new generation to the beauty of rosemaling. Today, this exuberant painting tradition continues to thrive in America, a reminder of the hand-wrought wonders that once graced Europe's humblest homes.

In a contemporary Illinois kitchen, a newly decorated chest (above) and painted cabinets (right) reflect the curvilinear forms and deep, vivid hues of rosemaling. The legend on the boxed beam reads, "Welcome to our home."

MEXICO AND CENTRAL AMERICA

When Hernando Cortez laid siege to Mexico and northern Central America in the 16th century, Roman Catholicism and pre-Columbian spiritualism met head on. The commingling of ornate Spanish baroque designs with native materials and motifs gave rise to a new form of folk art characterized by bold, brilliant color and an exuberant spirit. The serious religious sculpture of Roman Catholic Europe found new life as the ebullient, almost joyful, carved and painted *santos* (saints) of the New World.

Encouraged by Spanish missionaries who established programs to teach crafts and Catholic iconography to native populations, Mexicans embraced Christianity, but always in their own spirited fashion. The exotic and the mysterious continue to pervade Mexican folk art, ranging from fabulous nativity scenes to miniature skeletal musicians; crafted of clay and papier-mâché, these mystical band members appear each autumn on the Day of the Dead, when Mexicans pay tribute to their ancestors.

As they have for generations, many contemporary

folk artists favor indigenous materials, including plant fibers, earth, bone, and stone. Mexico's ubiquitous ceramic pots, for example, are traditionally fashioned from ground clay mixed with water, and kneaded by hand or foot—just as it has been for centuries.

Another survivor of pre-Columbian times is the gourd rattle—a staple of roving mariachi bands—which dates back to 6500 B.C., when bottle gourds were first cultivated in what is now Central America. Painstakingly applied layers of natural oils, powders, and pastes produce the luminous lacquer finish that makes each rattle an original work of art.

Today the spontaneity and vigor that typify Mexican folk art draw enthusiastic collectors. Piggy banks and clay-pot piñatas choked with toys, which have delighted children for generations, find a place of honor in homes throughout the Southwest and beyond. Tinwork mirrors and silver ornaments lend sparkle to mantels and hallways. And handmade ceramics, including the familiar, intensely colored Mexican floor and wall tiles, remain a well-loved addition to kitchens and patios everywhere.

Made in the 1920s and 1930s, clay banks shaped like corn, chilis, and fruit (opposite top) encouraged Mexican children to save their centavos. Glazed clay figures (opposite bottom) represent common occupations. A fully equipped kitchen (above), displayed at the Museum of International Folk Art in Santa Fe, typifies the miniature clay scenes still made in Mexico today. Tiny treasures include everything from mole pots to ceramic mugs.

NATIVE AMERICAN

Collectors have coveted Native American artifacts ever since 1804, when Lewis and Clark returned from their famous Western expedition and presented an elaborately decorated buffalo robe to President Thomas Jefferson, who had sponsored their journey. Then, as now, native crafts were valued for their warm, down-to-earth colors and textures, with patterns distinguished by a pleasing symmetry.

Native folk art of North America often showed an intriguing crossover of indigenous customs and influences introduced by white settlers. Early crafts were made with the materials at hand. In the Midwest, where grass was plentiful, for example, Plains Indians excelled at basket making. In the sun-baked Southwest, where the most abundant natural resource was the earth itself, Pueblo tribes became master potters. Tribes of the densely forested Northwest, including the Tlingit, Tsimshian, and Bellabella, carved totem poles and other sacred objects from wood, while farther north, Eskimos turned out delicate rattles shaped from walrus teeth.

As new materials came to Indian communities via traders, they were often used in unexpected ways.

Carved and painted totem poles (above) crown a late-1800s cupboard. Inside, baskets wear the graphic patterns typical of Native American design. Open palms on this silk-and-taffeta ceremonial blanket (left), made by the Osage Indians of the southeastern Plains, indicate that the wearer bears no weapons.

examples were produced by many tribes. The Apache, for example, are known for beautiful jarlike baskets called *ollas*, made by sewing together coiled bunches of plant materials, such as willow and cottonwood. *Ollas* could take up to a year to complete and were so tightly woven they could be used to carry water.

Today the legacy of Native American design is evident in such tribal artifacts as blankets, baskets, beadwork, and rattles, as well as in the bold geometric shapes and earthen hues frequently borrowed for contemporary quilts, printed textiles, and even china.

Artisans who were paid with silver coins—which served no purpose in tribal society—melted them down and reshaped the metal into jewelry. Commercially made cloth was painstakingly unraveled and rewoven into blankets and rugs.

Weaving, in fact, was a skill perfected by many tribes. The finest rugs and blankets now displayed by collectors originally served as overcoats and are the direct descendants of the *saltillos*, or ponchos, worn by Mexicans. After relying on indigenous materials for centuries, Pueblo women, who learned to weave from the Mexicans, began using wool from sheep brought to the New World by Spaniards; eventually, commercially dyed yarns also became available.

As frontier trading posts were set up, rugs and blankets became an important source of revenue. In general, designs produced for trade outside the Indian community were brighter in color and looser in weave than those created by Native Americans for their own use. Perhaps most eagerly sought today are Navajo Chief's blankets, whose patterns evolved over time from broad bands to stripes and diamonds. Baskets also played an important role in daily life, and superior

Beaded pincushions shaped like high-button shoes (above left) were probably made by a New England tribe and sold as souvenirs. Draped over a sofa back, a mid-19th-century Navajo textile (above right) displays the vivid colors of commercially dyed wool yarns produced in Germantown, Pennsylvania, and sold to Indians by traders. A coiled clay bowl crafted by New Mexico's Santa Domingo Indians sits next to a pair of beaded Sioux moccasins. Native American blankets, rugs, and baskets create a distinctive decor in a log cabin (overleaf).

SHAKER

Some of America's most beautiful and enduring folk art was created by members of early communal settlements. Among the most familiar of these groups are the Shakers, or the United Society of Believers in Christ's Second Appearing, a religious sect founded in England in the 18th century. In 1774 the Shakers set sail for America in order to escape the persecution engendered by their unusual worship rituals, which included self-induced trances, tongue-speaking, and the ecstatic dancing that earned them their name.

By 1850, some 20 Shaker communities were flourishing from New England to Indiana. Largely self-sufficient, the Shakers were a celibate sect that restricted their dealings with the outside world. They did, however, engage in some commerce to raise money to buy land for new settlements and proved to be especially canny business people. The Shakers were the first in America to package seeds commercially, and sold medicinal herbs, ointments, and wintergreen lozenges. Shaker-made brooms, baskets, and ladder-back chairs were also in high demand by the public.

Under a hierarchy led by elders and eldresses, all tasks undertaken by the extended Shaker "family"

were assigned according to age, strength, and ability. Shaker brothers did heavy field work and served as carpenters and furniture joiners. The Shaker sisters had their own workshops where they braided rugs and

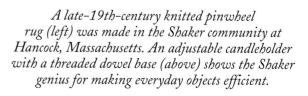

A late-19th-century knitted pinwheel rug (left) was made in the Shaker community at Hancock, Massachusetts. An adjustable candleholder with a threaded dowel base (above) shows the Shaker genius for making everyday objects efficient.

horsewhips, carded wool, spun thread, and made their famous palm bonnets and hats.

Believers first and craftsmen second, the Shakers were motivated by the words of their spiritual leader, Mother Ann Lee, who decreed, "Put your hands to work and your hearts to God." Their fine crafts evolved out of the belief that a design could always be bettered; utility came first and beauty followed as a result. The constant effort to improve the function of a piece accounted for the great variety of Shaker furnishings. These included sewing desks, efficient storage cupboards, and ingenious chairs that canted backwards or had ball-and-socket feet to permit their occupants to tilt back for more comfortable sitting.

Eager to reduce the effort spent on mundane tasks to allow more time for worship, the Shakers also continually improved their systems of heating,

refrigeration, lighting, and housekeeping. They were responsible for inventing the first washing machine, an automatic pea-sheller, the revolving oven, the circular saw, and—woe to us all—the alarm clock.

In the end, however, it is for their architecture and finely crafted furnishings that we remember the Shakers best. The Shaker eye for order and balance yielded buildings of near perfect symmetry, while capable hands turned out austerely beautiful quilts, rugs, and furniture with a grace of line and purity of form that has proved timeless.

A yellow-painted Shaker washstand (left) has a built-in candle shelf. Crafted of seasoned maple and pine, pantry boxes (above) feature deeply arched "fingers" to avoid splits; they originally held flour, sugar, and other kitchen staples. The yarn winder, or swift, to their right fastens onto a table for support.

LIVING WITH
FOLK ART

Simply put, living with folk art is a pleasure. Rooms decorated with woven coverlets, hooked rugs, painted furniture, decoys, and other handmade objects are naturally comfortable and welcoming; they immediately invite friends and family to relax and feel at home.

Why? One reason is the warmth and character in works of folk art, which are inherently less formal than high-style antiques. Imperfection, in fact, is often cause for celebration; the chips, nicks, worn paint, and broken threads that come with generations of use serve only to enhance individuality and interest. Each piece has its own story to tell and any "flaws" are merely chapters in the intriguing tale.

Because every work is special, it doesn't take a lot of folk art to make a statement. One stunning textile or a single sculptural basket may be all a room needs, especially if the object is displayed in relief against a backdrop of stark white walls.

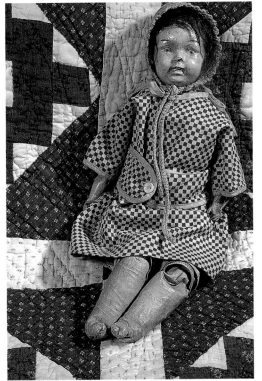

Folk art is also remarkably adaptable: A humble patchwork quilt can look right at home on a formal Regency bed, for example, while a collection of graceful shore-bird decoys arranged on glass shelves in a window will keep congenial company with the most contemporary of furnishings.

Appropriately, there are no hard and fast rules for collecting folk art. Some people choose to concentrate on a single material or genre—pottery, say, or portraits. Others might focus on the work of a particular ethnic group, such as Amish quilts. Still others move instinctively toward whatever catches their eye and interest.

However you go about collecting, learning about the background of a piece will enrich the experience. Where was it made, and of what materials? Who crafted it, and under what circumstances? Answers to such questions will not only increase value, should you ever want to sell a piece, but also will enhance your own enjoyment and understanding of folk art.

With its natural warmth, folk art mixes well with other types of collectibles. In a Victorian farmhouse (opposite), a rare crib-size Amish quilt in the graphic Railroad Crossing pattern sets off an Art Deco figure on the mantel. Italian grape-cluster lights and rugs hooked in the 1920s complete the eclectic decor. Sometimes a single great find, such as a well-loved kidskin doll (above), featuring painted blue eyes, is all it takes to bring a room interest.

ENTRIES
AND
HALLS

First impressions count. For this reason, home-owners have always been aware of how important a front entry or hall is, both in conveying a feeling of welcome and setting the stage for the rest of the house. In the American Colonies, this was true even in the earliest years of settlement; valued furnishings such as an heirloom chair or bench held a place of honor by the door, while a prized painting or mirror would hang on the wall.

Sometimes walls splashed with stenciled designs or panoramic murals met the eye. Or, a hooked rug might

warm a scrupulously clean, highly polished floor. Whatever treasures a family chose to display, entries provided an opportunity to make a statement about personal style and worldly accomplishment. Here was a place for the successful sea captain or merchant, for example, to show that his was no ordinary household.

Today these small spaces are still an ideal spot to usher in guests with an eye-catching touch—be it stenciled stair risers, an unusual carpet, or a conveniently placed bench.

The front hall in a Vermont house (overleaf) features whimsical beasts by a contemporary craftsman. A 1940s rag-rug runner (above left), hooked from dyed rayon stockings and wool scraps, sends a colorful welcome to guests; another rug (above right) conveys the same message. A carved cupboard with tombstone panels, topped by a toy truck and an Amish quilt in the Variable Star pattern, make a striking display for a small area at the foot of the staircase.

*A cigar-store Indian (above) greets visitors to a 1920s mountain camp
in the Adirondack region of upstate New York. Designed to entice customers into a tobacco
emporium, shop figures representing Native Americans were a symbol of good will.
Sometimes mounted on wheels, the wooden figures were brought indoors at night
and eventually became permanent indoor fixtures in response to complaints of crowded
sidewalks. Now they can find a welcome place in virtually any room of the house.*

LIVING WITH FOLK ART

3 3

PAINTED WALLS

Hiring an artist to embellish your home with decorative wall painting may seem extravagant today, but in the 18th and 19th centuries the practice actually made good economic sense. For country folk, painted murals and stenciling captured the color and pattern of the fine imported wallpapers that decorated fancy city houses—at a fraction of the cost.

Among the best known of the enterprising artists who offered their services door-to-door is Rufus Porter, a renaissance man who also worked as a shoemaker, schoolteacher, silhouette cutter, dancing master, and sign and drum painter. Porter took to the road as an artist around 1825, making stops at more than a hundred houses from Maine to Virginia. Worked directly on dry plaster walls, Porter's richly colored murals were composites of real and imaginary scenes. As he later revealed in the first issue of *Scientific American*, which he founded in 1845, Porter made liberal use of transfers, stencils, and cork stamps. These tools helped the artist achieve realistic images and, importantly, sped up the painting process. Porter claimed that for ten dollars an entire parlor or dining room could be painted in about five hours.

One of the other artists who worked with stencils was Moses Eaton. During the first half of the 19th century, Eaton traveled the countryside with a well-stocked pattern box and a selection of flat-head brushes, decorating everything from bedrooms to halls. Stencils were especially versatile, for they could be applied in all-over patterns, in friezes and borders, and in vertical bands used to break up large wall expanses.

With their homespun charm, murals and stenciling

transcend time and convey the character and individuality inherent in a country decor. Of course, early artists had to mix their own pigments, usually thinned with skim milk or—in the case of lampblack—with rum and water. Now, precut stencils and special paints are readily available, making it easy for anyone to share in this deeply rooted American folk art tradition.

As did early itinerant painters, today's muralists
often customize their work to include favorite themes or familiar views.
A contemporary mural (above) by California artist Mark Moss features a lone
pig in its pen, reflecting the homeowner's fondness for all things porcine. Artist
Michael Stiles painted the living-room walls of a restored New York State
farmhouse (opposite) with a view of nearby Otsego Lake .

*A remodeled 80-year-old parsonage (opposite) features stenciling copied
from Early American patterns and applied by the homeowners themselves. The colors
echo the hues in a collection of old stoneware, displayed underneath a contemporary
painting of Noah's ark done on old floorboards. The rounded mountain and
feathery trees of a new mural in a Kennebunkport, Maine, townhouse (above)
recall the work of the 19th-century itinerant artist Rufus Porter.*

BENCHES

Long and narrow, benches are shaped much like the halls and corridors they often serve. At their most practical, they provide convenient places to don and doff boots and outerwear, but they also make handsome display areas for folk art textiles such as quilts and coverlets, which may be draped across the arm or back of even the simplest piece for a dramatic effect.

Essential and functional, the bench was a common furniture type in the earliest days of Colonial settlement. Country craftsmen often based their work on high-style pieces whose designs originated in Europe, freely combining different stylistic features—as in the

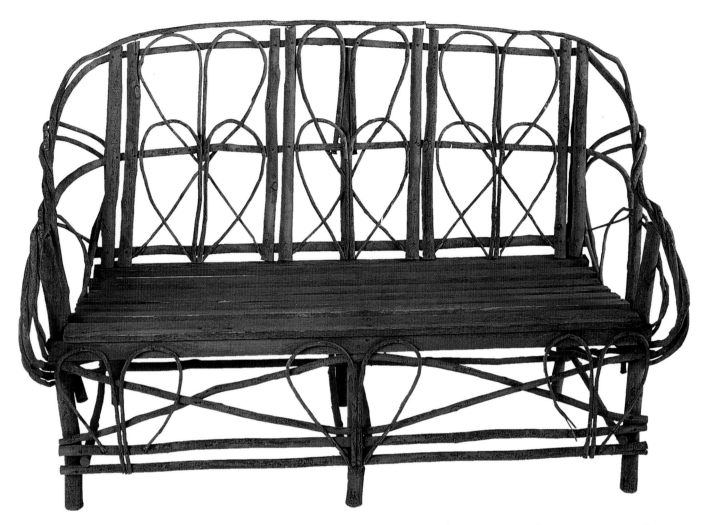

curved Queen Anne arms and broad-slatted Regency back of the painted piece shown opposite.

The style and shape of a bench depended on the size of an entrance hall as well as the depth of a homeowner's pockets. A very early bench type, called a form—consisting of a simple plank seat on plain legs—might serve a modest home. The first cousin of the form was the high-backed settle, a medieval furniture type that prevailed well into the 1700s. Well-established households might boast a more comfortable (and expensive) settee, essentially an extended armchair offering a generous seat and an angled back more conducive to lounging.

In today's country hallway, a church pew, schoolroom bench, bent-willow settee, or even a buggy seat might easily find a home near the front or back door. Grouped with other pieces, they can become the focal point of a folk art display, perhaps with paintings and a peg rack mounted above. Or a bench can simply be a sign of welcome, inviting visitors to stop and stay awhile.

Showing a soft patina from years of wear, a handsome painted bench (opposite) is now retired from active service and used for display. Dolls crafted by Florida's Seminole Indians take a seat alongside a 1900s crazy quilt and a piece of salt-glazed stoneware. Rustic benches like this distinctive bentwood willow-and-pine settee (above) typically featured knots and other irregularities. The piece remained in the same family from the 1920s to the 1980s.

LIVING
ROOMS

The living room as we know it today is a relative newcomer to the American home, appearing for the first time around the 1860s. Before then, most middle- and upper-class families welcomed guests in a formal reception room or front parlor; the more casual back parlor, or drawing room (originally "withdrawing room") was for everyday use.

Whereas the front parlor was used to show off the household's finest furniture, the back parlor was the hub of daily activity. Here lessons were learned, letters written, games played, and the day's events discussed. A desk often filled one corner and a daybed another.

As houses and parlors grew smaller in the early 20th century, the front parlor became a little used luxury few could afford, and the "living room" was born. Combining the casualness of the drawing room and the "best" side of the old front parlor, the new room became the setting for get-togethers both formal and informal.

As a gathering place, the living room is a natural showcase for family treasures. Portraits and stenciled theorem paintings, pottery, and textiles all look their best in this comfortable space where prized possessions and favorite collections can be admired and even touched.

A collection of folk art, including seaweed-patterned yellowware pitchers, anniversary-tin utensils, and a theorem painting of fruit, makes a simply furnished country living room (overleaf) come alive. Setting shore-bird and duck decoys on glass window shelves (above) shows off the graceful silhouettes of these wood carvings. A weather vane with an especially graphic profile sits atop a mantel in a room filled with grain-painted pieces (opposite).

BASKETS

Characterized by an admirable blend of form and function, baskets have long attracted collectors with their satisfying textures and natural materials. Baskets boast a long and rich history that also enhances their interest. In America these utilitarian handcrafts served the households of Native Americans and European settlers alike. Many types, such as the open-weave cheese drainer, were designed for food preparation; others were intended to transport all manner of goods, from eggs to firewood. Still other baskets served for storing food and household items.

Invariably, a basket featured a logical design; the weave and shape—and the size of the handle, bottom, and edges—were governed by the weight and type of objects the piece was to hold. A tobacco basket, for example, had an open weave necessary for drying large leaves. Nut and berry baskets, by contrast, were small and densely woven to preserve moisture. Large splint baskets were used for carrying heavier loads, such as apples, potatoes, and corn. By distributing weight to the sides, smaller baskets with raised centers prevented eggs from breaking and peaches from bruising. Elongated baskets made handy eel traps.

If in good condition, vintage baskets can still find uses in today's households. Tobacco baskets may display blankets and linens. Tightly woven berry baskets store jewelry and buttons, while lidded baskets are often used to hold herbs or potpourri.

Fragile by nature, however, all baskets deserve special care and handling. It is always a good idea to lift an old basket by the base or sides since the handle may no longer be strong. Direct sunlight and heat are also

harmful, as is excessive moisture; for this reason an antique basket should never be used to hold a plant.

Astute collectors seek examples with as few repairs as possible, as these are the baskets that will retain their value. Perhaps most eagerly hunted are decorated baskets, such as those stamped with designs cut from potatoes and other vegetables.

A corner cupboard bearing blue milk paint showcases a varied basket collection (above). The lidded baskets were crafted by Native Americans, who often dyed the splints before weaving. Made primarily in the 19th and early 20th centuries, those decorated with potato stamping and freehand designs were sold as souvenirs. Fingerlap storage boxes share the center shelf with early factory-made toys.

*A wide assortment of baskets lends texture and warmth to a rustic
living room (above). Shelves hold numerous egg baskets; more unusual types include
a fishing creel, mounted on the wall by the window, and a Nantucket lightship
basket—on the table—notable for its close weave and articulated handle. Baskets find
an equally welcome home in a more contemporary living room (overleaf), where
they come in handy for holding books and an armful of dried bittersweet.*

PORTRAITS

Before photography became relatively widespread in the late 1800s, Americans relied on portraits to preserve their likenesses for posterity. These artworks reveal far more than the facial characteristics of a particular individual. Through oil paintings and watercolors, silhouettes, and miniatures we can gauge the attitudes of an era. Occupations, fashions, and important events of the day, along with clues to social standing and educational achievements, were all recorded by self-taught artists.

Often subjects were portrayed with props or in embellished settings. These were sometimes incorporated at the artist's whim, but usually added at the specific request of the sitter. Jewelry and expensive

clothing, for example, communicated material success, as did fine furnishings or a view of extensive farm-land from a window. A book held in hand or dis-played on a table was sometimes meant to indicate literacy, a significant achievement in the 18th and early 19th centuries. In the case of a gentleman, a book's title might also reveal his livelihood; a pastor, for instance, would typically hold a Bible.

America's earliest portraits, which date to the 17th century, are not truly representative of the sitter. Concerned with clothing and accessories, most paint-ings were more likely to signify wealth and social position than to record an exact likeness. Portraits commissioned in the next century, on the other hand, often show a more sincere attempt to capture the actual features and personality of the subject. By this time, the market for portraits had extended beyond the aristocracy to include the middle class, creating a demand for more folk artists, or limners, as they were known. Sometimes itinerants, these resourceful artists frequently traveled hundreds of miles from home in search of new commissions.

Because limners viewed themselves more as craftsmen than artists, they seldom signed their work.

In a handsome living room (opposite), portraits are set off against a simple white background and highlighted with track lighting. The style of the gentleman's black tie indicates that the husband-and-wife pair dates from the 1830s or 1840s. The likeness over the fireplace was done earlier, when white stock collars were still in vogue. A manteltop portrait in a snug living room (above) fits with a mix of pewter, stoneware, and toys.

Collectors of folk art portraits thus need to attribute their paintings through other means. Details repeated in one painting to the next—the same fabric pattern, for instance—sometimes identify a particular artist. Dating involves similar guesswork. Looking at clothing and hair styles is a good way to determine the period in which a portrait was done. Other elements used as artistic devices, such as ships in a distant view, also help narrow down a time period.

Unlike schooled artists, who were able to charge high rates, folk painters were often obliged to engage in other occupations when commissions grew scarce.

As oil portraits averaged 20 dollars apiece and paper silhouettes were priced at two for 25 cents, portraiture was occasionally a means to supplement regular incomes from farming, taxidermy, and sign painting. However, in 1839, Samuel F. B. Morse, a painter-turned-inventor, introduced Americans to a French invention called the daguerreotype, and the days were soon numbered for folk portraitists.

Fast, inexpensive, and accurate, the new photographs offered distinct advantages to painted portraits. Some folk painters decided not to even try to compete and simply opened photography studios.

Individual husband-and-wife portraits painted to face each
other, as this couple (above) do, are known as pendant pairs. The lady's
red book, a prop commonly used in such paintings, may indicate the
sitter was educated. Folk artists were obliged to work quickly in order to earn
a living; by repeating accessories and poses from painting to painting,
these limners were able to increase their speed and productivity.

Others attempted to promote the virtues of paintings over black-and-white photography: A painted work was not only done in color but also could be as large as the customer desired, whereas photographs were necessarily small. The fact that deceased or otherwise absent family members could always be added to a painting was another important advantage. By the 1860s, however, photography had won the contest and folk painters had to find other ways to make a living.

Today folk art portraits are appreciated for—rather than in spite of—their lack of technical expertise. The best examples show a power of observation and sense of design often unmatched in the works of trained artists. Even when the figure is an anonymous sitter whose name is long forgotten, such works are fascinating references to the past, with a mystery and appeal that complement any room.

If period frames are not available, portraits may be effectively displayed unframed, since compelling images will always hold their own. No painting should be exposed to direct sunlight, which can fade colors and weaken the paint.

*A striking image of a woman mounted over a living-room
fireplace (above) reflects the fine hand of an academically trained painter, while
the picture over the sofa shows the unschooled approach of a genuine folk artist.
A pair of full-length watercolor portraits (overleaf) are by Jacob Mantel,
an immigrant farmer from Germany who worked as a folk artist in Pennsylvania
and Indiana. Mantel died in 1863 at the age of 100.*

WEATHER VANES

Like so many folk art forms, weather vanes were practical as well as decorative. No farmer was without one of these useful wind indicators; it was common knowledge in any Eastern Colony that if a vane pointed east it would soon be time to take shelter, for rain was on the way.

But vanes did more than indicate wind direction. They were also eye-catching sculptures whose forms often announced their location. When positioned like a sentinel atop a barn, for example, a well-fed cow might indicate dairy production, while a robust ram could serve as a mascot for a wool factory. As a steeple's crowning glory, a vane in the form of the archangel Gabriel summoned one and all to church, as did a vane shaped like a fish, an ancient symbol of Christianity.

Ship weather vanes sailed high above houses in seaport towns, and sleek steeds pranced above stables devoted to harness racing, America's most popular sport by the mid-19th century. As symbols of brotherhood, weather vanes depicting Indian chiefs, in turn, often stood atop the roofs of clubhouses and civic buildings.

A rare horse vane (left) dates from the early 1800s; few all-wood pieces such as this survive. A circa 1870 sailboat (above) hails from the shop of L.W. Cushing of Massachusetts, a prominent 19th-century weather vane manufacturer. Perhaps made for a boathouse, the piece features traces of the original gilt detailing.

Although the weather vane originated in Europe, the form found its greatest artistic expression in America. Handmade weather vanes were generally of wood, carved flat or in three dimensions, or forged from iron. Beginning in the mid-1850s, factories began turning out hollow-cast vanes made from copper or zinc hammered into a mold. Wooden vanes seldom survived the elements for long and today are rare indeed. Hand-forged vanes lasted longer, and can be seen in museums; rare examples also appear in private collections.

Most of the weather vanes surviving today are the factory-made examples, which were originally sold through catalogues for about 35 dollars apiece. Examples dating to the 1800s, however, are now so scarce that the chances of stumbling on one in an old barn or at an estate sale are increasingly slim.

The best weather vanes show a sense of natural movement in their forms—as in a jumping horse or a running dog with its tail flying behind. These sculptural pieces are best placed up high, atop a cupboard or fireplace mantel, for example, so they can be seen from below as originally intended. Most vanes are now sold already mounted on bases, which should be as plain and unobtrusive as possible.

An 1880s sulky and driver (above) trot atop a 1790
Pennsylvania German cupboard known as a schrank. Mounted on a
narrow base made of pine, this striking weather vane is seen
to advantage from below. A handsome vane displayed above a brick bake
oven (overleaf) may represent St. Tammany, the legendary chief of the
Delawares who was revered for his eloquence and courage.

*The unwitting victim of target practice,
a horse weather vane (above) still has plenty of charm.
A hollow-cast ram (right) reigned over a New England
sheep farm. A pair of horse weather vanes (opposite)
are a natural fit in a converted barn; the fish is a form
that often topped a church steeple.*

SHIPS AND FISH

As an important source of food, travel, and commerce, the country's waterways figured prominently in early American life and were a constant and natural source for folk art themes. Among the legacies of America's early romance with the water are models of all kinds of seaworthy craft.

Rooted in a tradition going as far back as the Elizabethan era, models built to scale enabled a boat-builder to test the proportions and lines of a ship while providing a "picture" of the finished product for his client. Ships' captains displayed these models as mementos of past and future achievement. Models

Colorful fishing lures equipped with hooks (above) create a three-dimensional display in an old shadow box. Swimming along a wall (opposite), ice-fishing decoys include both fish and frogs. Such decoys, including pike, trout, and perch, were made by both professional carvers and amateur fishermen. They generally date from the 1920s to the 1950s and often come from the Great Lakes region of Michigan, Minnesota, and Wisconsin.

continued to be made for steamboats, which had revolutionized the shipping industry by the 1840s. Quick to capitalize on the public's fascination with steam-powered vessels, toymakers were also soon turning out miniature watercraft—often exact replicas of the larger versions.

Also popular among collectors are gaily colored fish decoys and lures made of painted wood. Used in freshwater ice fishing, weighted decoys in the shape of fish and frogs were attached by a line to a pole called a jigging stick, then lowered into the water through a hole cut in the ice. Once the fish were attracted into range by the decoys, they could be speared from above. Lures, by contrast, were made with hooks and used on fishing poles, snaring unsuspecting prey by mimicking minnows and other bait.

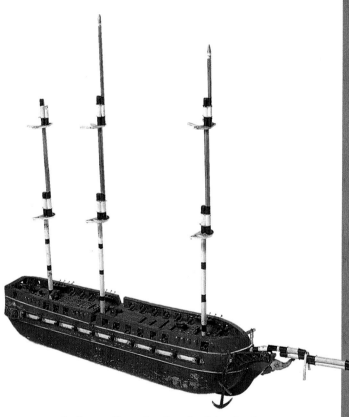

An intact figurehead and original paint finish distinguish a seafaring ship's model (above), built after World War II. Victor, a hand-carved tugboat, chugs along a refectory table (right); the stick-mounted fish was originally a weather vane. Another vessel is shown off in the bay window.

TOYS

Playthings have a fascinating history; besides telling us how children occupied themselves through the centuries, toys reveal the values and concerns of parents and of a community at large, illustrating the importance attached to material objects, social conventions, and new technology.

For the children of America's early Colonists, childhood was spent on household tasks and school-work, with little if any time left for play. Calvinist doctrine frowned on idle hands, and parents knew that youngsters who lacked basic skills had little chance of succeeding as adults. Treated like miniature grown ups, children in the 1600s and early 1700s had few toys indeed.

As the 18th century progressed, the burden on children began to ease and they found an increasing

Created in response to children's preference for playthings with movable parts, articulated toys have long been popular. A 20th-century piece (above) features dancing couples that rotate when the brightly painted toy is pushed or pulled.

number of outlets for their boundless energy and imagination. So-called Sunday toys offered education and quiet amusement on the Sabbath, when active play was often strictly forbidden. Perhaps the best known of these treasures are Noah's arks, gaily colored and stocked with beasts most youngsters would never see in storybooks or zoos. Also permissible on Sundays were educational toys such as alphabet blocks, sometimes painted in schemes of red, white, and blue.

Favorite playthings also included wooden animals and other familiar figures lovingly carved by relatives and friends; some of these early toys can be seen in folk art portraits of the late 18th and early 19th centuries. Dolls were also frequently made at home from rags, wood, nuts, dried apples, cornhusks, and even twigs. Perhaps the most common type were cloth dolls, readily born of the fabric scraps saved by all thrifty families and showing off the sewing skills essential to every young lady's education.

Stuffed with rags, straw, or sawdust, many cloth dolls wore clothing stitched directly onto their bodies. Doll hair might be created from yarn, thread, corn silk, human or horsehair, or animal fur. When properly dressed, even the occasional bedpost fragment or

Begging to be touched, a pair of teddies by
the fireplace, ninepins, and model aircraft lend a relaxed spirit to the
living room of an 1892 Queen Anne–style home in North Carolina (above).
As Americans became increasingly fascinated with new developments
in transportation technology, toymakers capitalized on the interest by making
boats, autos, and airplanes in miniature form.

clothespin might make a handsome doll. While faces were generally drawn or stitched, some figures wore no expression at all: Believing it heretical to portray or behold the human countenance, the Amish made their dolls without facial features.

Homemade cloth dolls remained popular as late as 1914, when a little girl named Marcella Gruelle found an old rag doll in her family's Indianapolis attic. Marcella took the faceless plaything (presumably made by Marcella's great-grandmother) to her father, the artist and writer Johnny Gruelle. With a few sure strokes of his pen, Gruelle gave the toy a one-line smile and triangular nose, then added a pair of button eyes.

Marcella named her new dolly Raggedy Ann, after characters in poems by John Whitcomb Riley, a family friend. Although Marcella died in 1917, Raggedy Ann lived on, in more than 20 books written and illustrated by Marcella's father and in countless dolls sewed by her

by her mother and aunt. Among the most popular dolls of all time, Raggedy Ann (and her pal Andy) are still duplicated by resourceful home sewers across the country.

Rivaling dolls in popularity were toys that moved in some way. Carved or stuffed animals were fun, but pull toys with articulated parts or attached to wheels were irresistible. Rocking horses and barnyard beasts with mouths that opened also held great appeal. Balancing toys fascinated generations of youngsters; these generally featured a clown or other figure whose center of gravity was fixed with weighted balls.

Whirligigs, too, offered the thrill of movement. These wind toys were possibly introduced to America by German immigrants in Pennsylvania.

Soberly dressed Amish dolls look right at home on the sofa of a log house living room (opposite). More cloth dolls rest comfortably in an antique doll bed. Like many 19th-century toys, alphabet blocks (above left) were intended to instruct as well as amuse; the homemade dolly features a hand-drawn face. An early battery-powered toy, the Ferris wheel (above right) celebrates America's longtime love affair with amusement parks.

Whirligigs were carved from solid blocks of wood or assembled from individual pieces cut from a board. Complex examples with numerous parts were powered by pinwheel-like propellers that caught the wind and spun around. Gears and connecting rods activated the figure, which might represent a soldier or policeman, or even Uncle Sam. Most were mounted outdoors on fenceposts where, like weather vanes, they could be used to gauge wind velocity; watching an authoritarian figure such as a policeman aimlessly flail his arms no doubt added to the appeal of such pieces.

By the 19th century, amusements were increasingly shared by both adults and children. Board games, dominoes, cards, darts, and dice were all popular. Board games, in particular, were widespread by 1850. While checkers predominated, other popular pastimes included pachisi, backgammon, and Chinese checkers; some reversible boards offered a different game on each side. Although professional sign painters occasionally embellished boards with such motifs as vines and flowers, many early examples were created by home craftsmen working with basic tools and recycled

Game boards lend their graphic patterns to
white walls in a casual living room (overleaf). The large lozenge-shaped
checkerboard displayed to the right of the fireplace was designed
to rest on two players' knees. Pull toys, rocking horses, and
miniature buildings bring a whimsical touch to a vacation house (above).
The quilt was pieced from calico and sack cloth.

wood, such as old breadboards. As the century progressed, toys mirrored outstanding scientific and industrial advancements. Miniature trains had entered the nursery almost as soon as the first iron horse made headlines in the 1830s. Toy Ferris wheels heralded the late–Victorian passion for amusement parks (the first full-size Ferris wheel appeared in 1892). Model gliders and airplanes crafted in home workshops commemorated the Wright brothers' successful flight on December 17, 1902. The horseless carriage, another early-20th-century marvel, was also widely interpreted by amateur and professional toymakers alike.

These days, such one-of-a-kind playthings have left the playroom and become showpieces in the living room, where they lend their sculptural shapes and playful spirit to coffee tables, mantelpieces, and shelves. Whether displayed as a collection or individually, toys can transform an otherwise unremarkable room into an engaging, whimsical haven.

An 1870s shelf made of discarded spools (top) holds polychrome blocks, Russian spheres, and, on the top shelf, a cache of Mennonite and Amish balls; some of them are playthings, others are pincushions. Now cleverly mounted on a sheet-metal base, a rare cast-iron carnival dog (above) once did time in a shooting gallery. A doll's quilt (overleaf) hangs from a playhouse porch. Sometimes as small as 12 inches square, doll quilts were frequently stitched by little girls learning to sew.

SIGNS AND ADVERTISING

Painted signs were the earliest form of advertising in Colonial America, used to identify shops and services and to advise weary travelers where they might obtain refreshment or put up for the night. Since many people could not read, most signs conveyed their messages with pictures: A soldier or sailor raising a tankard of ale, for example, was difficult to misinterpret. Similarly, signs for professional scribes, who penned documents for illiterate clients, typically bore the image of a large quill pen.

In the late 18th and 19th centuries, improved manufacturing methods for all manner of goods meant greater competition, and advertising became increasingly important. Sending fast and immediate messages, three-dimensional images came on the scene. Pedestrians found it impossible to ignore a giant molar complete with roots dangling in front of the dentist's office, or a Goliath-size boot swinging next to a shoemaker's door. Oversize scissors (tailors' shops), giant eyeglasses (opticians' offices), and enormous pocket watches (retail and repair shops) fairly screamed for attention.

In time, however, most of these exaggerated show-stoppers vanished in the wake of changing technology. One that endured, however, was the barbershop pole, which has a long tradition of use in both Europe and America. Some historians speculate that the red spiral indicated the barber's status as a surgeon or bloodletter, services he might offer in addition to the occasional haircut and shave. A black stripe meant the proprietor doubled as an undertaker.

Another form of advertising, shop figures also enjoyed an extended reign, from about 1850 to 1900. Many wooden shop figures were the work of former ships' carvers who turned to the sign-making business when the shipbuilding industry began to decline in the mid-19th century. Craftsmen roughed out the

*Constructed of tin and measuring
28 inches high, an oversize hand (left) was designed
to advertise the wares of a glovemaker's shop.
Gold paint highlights the fingernails,
while a coat of white picks out a frilly sleeve
with a scalloped cuff.*

What may appear to be a country store (above) is actually an
Atlanta living room. Almost everything on display here dates from between
1880 and 1890, including the oak seed counter piled high with vintage
containers for kitchen staples, as well as advertising signs and graniteware,
a type of enameled metalware. The grain sacks, a biscuit box, and glass
display cases were collected for their advertising slogans.

With the 19th century came color lithography, and a new era in advertising began. This printing process made it possible to produce several hundred flawless impressions from a single master. Trade cards, signs, and product labels could thus be mass-produced and inexpensively distributed.

While their purpose was to advertise, wooden signs and printed ephemera were often beautifully crafted artworks as well. As a result, their visual interest has endured even when the product or service the sign was advertising has long disappeared.

figures, often using solid pine spars from shipyards, and worked out the fine details with a chisel.

These carvings, in the form of policemen, sailors, and even Scottish Highlanders, were placed outside shops to catch the eye of passersby. Of all the shop figures, however, the cigar-store Indian is most familiar. Native Americans had been identified with the exotic tobacco leaf ever since they introduced it to Europeans in the 1600s, and the Indian figure became a natural advertising symbol for a tobacco shop.

Mounted over a sofa, a prized hand-painted horse sign (opposite) was hung at the end of a farm lane. Featuring scroll carving and stenciling, an 1847 trade sign (above left) also depicts a horse. A giant eye (above right) once looked down from the ceiling of a meeting hall of the Independent Order of Odd Fellows, a benevolent society founded in 1819. The homemade telescope is crafted of cardboard, stained to look like leather.

HORSES

Long a symbol of wealth and social standing, the horse is one of the most frequently portrayed images in American folk art, celebrated by weather vanes, paintings, inn and tavern signs, hooked rugs, carvings, and children's toys. This familiar beast of burden was introduced to North and Central America by Spanish explorers in the 1500s, and Native Americans learned to rely on the horse early on.

For generations of children, the next-best thing to having a horse of one's own was knowing a rocking horse was waiting in the playroom. A handsome painted wooden pony (above) rocks back and forth on an arched runner. A more primitive version (opposite) boasts a horsehair tail and realistic leather reins.

Nineteenth-century blankets that depict the pony in profile represented the animal's importance to the Navajos, for example. For European settlers, the horse, which could pull heavy plows and help transport goods to market, made large-scale farming possible. Owning such an animal also represented the freedom to travel and to attend church and social functions in style.

Horses, however, were valued for more than their practical virtues. Before the Civil War, the animals became America's first sports heroes when racing fever took the country by storm. Racehorses represented financial success and social position. Any well-to-do gentleman worth his salt had at least one pacer or trotter in his stable, typically crowned by a weather vane showing a horse galloping at full throttle. Many horse vanes, in fact, were named for a particular trotter, such as the famous racehorses Ethan Allen and Black Hawk.

A doll-size rocking horse with a fuzzy mane joins a checkerboard atop a blanket chest (above). Displayed on a farm table (right), a rare rocking horse dating from the second half of the 19th century features a Windsor-style seat. Nearby, a miniature horse and cab cruise for a passenger.

WHIMSIES

While folk art is often functional as well as decorative, some pieces were created simply to pass the time, and for no other reason than to enchant and amuse. Most of these "whimsies" were sculptures, which might be born of any number of materials, including pottery, scrimshaw, molded plaster, carved wood, or pieced together from found objects such as bicycle parts and bottle caps.

In America the tradition of whittling animals from wood found rich expression as European immigrants with woodworking backgrounds traveled from village to village peddling their one-of-a-kind treasures. Some of these professional carvers are best known for a single design, such as an eagle or a rooster.

Many craftsmen also carved for the pure pleasure of it. One such artisan was the folk artist Fred K. Alten, of Wyandotte, Michigan, whose carving spanned the first four decades of this century. Working in his backyard shed, Alten carved hundreds of wooden animals, including exotic beasts as well as familiar domestic species. Only Alten's family knew of the woodworker's after-hours exploits, and his art went unnoticed after his death in 1945. Thirty years later, however, part of his menagerie was discovered by collectors who happened to walk into the folk artist's abandoned shed.

In addition to wood, chalkware—made from gypsum, the main ingredient in plaster of Paris—offered an inexpensive medium for decorative handcrafts. Chalkware figurines were issued in large quantities by manufacturers by the 19th century. Chalkware cats, dogs, parrots, flowers, and fruit were inexpensively cast

As a favorite subject of woodcarvers, animals take many folk art forms. A 1930s turtle footstool with stenciled markings (left) is one of a group made in graduated sizes. A remarkable "ball-in-cage" lion whimsey (above) was made from a single slab of wood, including the balls.

from molds, then gaily—even gaudily—painted. This poor man's answer to Staffordshire china adorned mantels and tabletops throughout the Victorian era.

Other whimsies include so-called end-of-day pieces, made by glass blowers, woodcarvers, and potters from scraps left over after the day's work was done. Glass blowers produced rolling pins and canes flamboyantly decorated with colorful spirals. Woodcarvers turned out toys, especially animals, to take home to their children, along with intricate boxes for their wives; potters, in turn, worked bits of clay into animals and other figures.

Working in a backyard shed in his spare time, day laborer
Fred Alten crafted an intriguing menagerie of prehistoric animals (above left) beginning
around 1915. A creative tour de force, a musical horn made around 1900 (above right)
was born of pewter spoons, stove parts, an insect sprayer, and a kazoo. Using local basswood,
from the linden tree, contemporary craftsman Stephen Huneck created an original
cast of characters (overleaf) for his Vermont home.

DINING ROOMS

Country dining has always had an informal character. In early Colonial days a table and chairs were usually kept against a wall and simply moved into the center of whatever room was convenient. It was not until the mid-1800s that a room reserved specifically for dining first came into fashion.

Today's country dining room is not only a place to linger over a cup of coffee or glass of wine, but can also be a handsome gallery for displaying prized folk art. Cupboards stocked with salt-glazed stoneware or red-ware, for example, look especially striking when bathed in candlelight, as do wildfowl decoys, baskets, and other treasures.

Moreover, the essential informality of folk art furnishings immediately sets guests at ease. Hooked rugs artfully arranged on a wall can be admired at leisure, their vivid tones and naïve images fully appreciated for the first or even the tenth time. And on the table itself, a 19th-century penny rug painstakingly stitched with bright felt circles becomes a conversation piece.

Set off by the neutral tones of an open-shelved cupboard,
a collection of redware is the focal point of a comfortable country dining
room (overleaf). The top-hatted shop figure, which once advertised a haberdashery,
was made in New England. Guarded by a a pair of Canada geese, an unusual
wall display (above) comprises a variety of maple-sugar molds, some in
the shapes of hearts and maple leafs.

In a Long Island, New York, weekend house (above),
early-20th-century trade signs and game boards dating from the 1800s
lend vitality and visual interest to a sparely decorated dining room.
A checkerboard-patterned woven rug and black Windsor chairs underscore
the room's simplicity, while rough-hewn beams, barn siding, and
textured plaster contribute warmth and a sense of history.

LIVING WITH FOLK ART

CUPBOARDS

These days, built-in closets can be counted on to fill most storage needs. In earlier times, however, dish cupboards and freestanding wardrobes offered the best, and often only, means of keeping order throughout the house. Elaborately painted or carved, some cupboards are works of art in themselves, and collectors avidly seek them out. Others, vintage country pieces turned mellow with age, provide the ideal setting in which to preserve and show off folk art collections.

Among the most distinctive early cupboard types were the folk forms brought to America by Northern European immigrants. Perhaps the best known are the Dutch kas (or *kast*) and the German schrank. Descended from the medieval linen press, these massive wardrobes were often ornately painted, not only to provide color and pattern in a room but also to disguise poor-quality wood or clumsy joinery. The kas was common in Dutch communities in the Hudson River valley and parts of Long Island and New Jersey. Usually set on enormous ball feet, it incorporated a space for hanging clothes as well as drawers for linens. The schrank, the prized possession of settlers from the German Palatinate, had a similar form, with interior shelves and pegs and double doors over drawers. These pieces reflect the woodworking and decorating skills for which the Germans are so highly regarded.

The commodious interiors of the kas and schrank make such large case pieces good places to house video and stereo equipment. When fitting an antique for a new use, it is important to do so with particular care to avoid damage. The couple who own the magnificent painted schrank illustrated on the opposite page, for example, expanded the storage space in their dining room by building a self-supporting set of shelves to fit neatly, and safely, inside the cupboard. In this way, they protected both an irreplaceable piece of American folk art as well as their own investment.

Dating from the early 1900s, an intricately inlaid cupboard (above) was inspired by a factory-made Hoosier cabinet, but crafted entirely by hand. It features a built-in clock, a pull-out cutting board, and a dozen tiny spice drawers. A grain-painted Pennsylvania German schrank (opposite) was built around 1800 and stayed in the maker's family for the next 150 years. The heavy cornice is typical of these massive wardrobes.

A later cupboard type popular among collectors is the "Hoosier," named after its Indiana origins. (The first was produced around 1900 by the Hoosier Manufacturing Company of Newcastle, Indiana.) From the early 1900s until about 1940, cooks relied on the ingeniously outfitted cabinets to store staples such as flour and sugar, along with cooking utensils and dishes; some pieces came equipped with built-in breadboards and tin-lined bread bins. While most Hoosiers were factory made, some were handcrafted folk copies of the store-bought models.

Glass doors on a pine cupboard
from Minnesota (above) ensure that a collection
of mochaware can always be seen. A painted
step-back cupboard (right) is at home in a converted
stable; the doors are left open to show off a display
of humble yet decorative yellowware.

BIRD DECOYS

Designed to attract waterfowl into hunting range, the decoy originated in this country with the Native Americans. Evidence shows that tribes in what is now Nevada were fashioning birdlike bundles of reeds and feathers to attract ducks and geese as early as a thousand years ago. The custom spread to the East Coast, where hunters placed small mounds of stones by the water's edge to imitate nesting ducks as a lure for mallards and other water birds.

Adopting this Native American innovation, European settlers refined the decoy, which derives its name from the Dutch *kooi*, a type of cage used to trap wildfowl. Carved from local woods—typically cedar, cypress, pine, or cottonwood—specific decoy types were developed according to the habits of a particular prey. The "stick-up" decoy, for example, was designed as either a flat or three-dimensional carving mounted on a pole; this was firmly planted in the mud, sand, or

A group of waterfowl decoys (opposite)
includes pieces ranging in date from the late 1800s to the 1930s.
The Canada goose on the bench features interchangeable male and female
heads sewn from socks. The miniature birds in a chest-top display (above)
are by Elmer Crowell. Perhaps the most famous of all decoy makers,
Crowell worked in Cape Cod in the early 1900s.

tall grass at the water's edge to attract shore birds such as curlews and plovers that frequent these areas.

Larger waterfowl, such as mallard, pintail, and canvasback ducks, which spend most of their time in the water, were best lured with floating decoys. These occasionally were made with hollow bodies that allowed them to float higher; lead weights nailed to the underside kept the carvings upright.

Because decoys were meant to provide a general impression of a particular bird, rather than be an exact replica, precise details such as feathers mattered little. Working decoys usually had highly stylized and even abstract designs, in contrast to the detailed carvings now produced as artworks. Decoys were often home-made, but there were also professional decoy makers who earned a name for themselves with beautifully carved works. Factories produced decoys as well.

Typically, a craftsman started with a well-aged block of wood—sometimes a piece of driftwood—roughing out a bird's basic shape with a jackknife.

The head, which was the most important element, was carved separately with help of a template or other pattern and attached with nails to the body. A simple paint finish helped preserve the wood, which was important, as some decoys might remain in the water throughout the entire hunting season.

Decoys were remarkably effective—so effective that by the dawn of the 20th century many bird species faced extinction. In 1918, under pressure from conservationists, Congress outlawed the shooting of wildfowl for commerical purposes, and the killing of shore birds was eventually banned altogether. While some decoys are still produced for duck hunters, most contemporary models are carved and painted as artworks.

Collectors of decoys both new and old look for exciting sculptural forms that suggest movement or potential flight. Some people are particularly interested in pieces with an original finish or those crafted by a specific maker, while others are simply drawn to a carving with inherent character that brings life to a room.

Stick-up decoys (above) include a long-beaked curlew;
the Maine plover to its right is designed to look as though it is swallowing
a minnow. The piece in the foreground is a robin snipe, while the floater
to the left is a coot with a head made from a root. Canada geese (opposite) make
an original display on a New England hutch table.

PAINTED CHAIRS

Bringing color and pattern into the home, painted chairs have long found a welcome place in country rooms. While examples painted in a single hue were originally relegated to the back porch, later versions embellished with stenciled or freehand designs, grain painting, and gilt decoration served proudly in the finest parlors. Exuberant and often breathtakingly pretty, painted chairs have been contributing grace and charm to American dining rooms since the early 1800s.

Windsors, perhaps America's first painted chairs, came to the New World in the 18th century from England, where they were used by the upper classes as outdoor furniture. Painted (typically green or black) as protection against the elements, these versatile chairs became ubiquitous in homes and taverns across the coun-

try. Over time, the shapes and colors of Windsor chairs grew more varied to meet changing tastes and needs, and boasted such refinements as rosewood graining.

Prevalent Windsor styles included the high-back (also called the comb-back), the low-back, and the sack-back (usually an armchair with an arched, braced back). Easily transported from room to room as the need for additional seating arose, well-used Windsors were frequently spruced up with a fresh coat of paint, making it difficult for today's collector to determine a chair's original color.

By 1800, other chairs began to make the early

In the hands of a master painter, even inexpensive woods
could be made glorious. An early-19th-century pine armchair (above left)
wears rosebuds on its crown and rail, as well as fancy gilding and black
pinstriping. Golden feathers adorn a rush-seated armchair (above right), which
features a delicately cut center splat. An arrow-back Windsor chair (opposite),
with decorated crest and spindles, hails from New England.

Windsors look tame. A rage for so-called fancy furniture—characterized by shimmering lacquered finishes and heavy use of gilt—encouraged craftsmen to set up workshops capable of turning out chairs highlighted in gold and bearing miniature landscapes on backsplats and crests. Like Windsors, fancy furniture came to America from England, where it was popularized by the 18th-century furniture designers Thomas Sheraton and George Hepplewhite. Fancy furniture was just that, and Americans couldn't get enough of it. In Baltimore alone, more than 50 makers advertised their services.

The first fancy chairs weren't cheap. At three dollars and fifty cents for a single chair decorated with

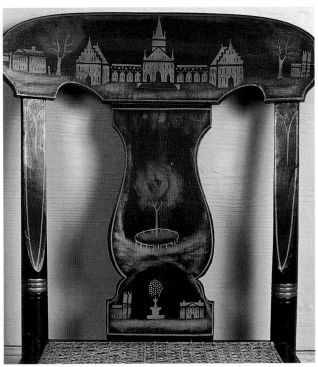

with gold leaf, most examples were available only to the fortunate few. In the 1820s, though, an entrepreneur named Lambert Hitchcock changed this situation dramatically. For a dollar and fifty cents, Hitchcock offered a well-made decorated chair that came with the word "warranted" marked on its underside, an early guarantee that the maker stood behind his product.

Hitchcock's three-story brick factory in the Connecticut village of Barkhamsted (later renamed Hitchcocksville and now known as Riverton) flourished, and a retail outlet was soon opened in nearby Hartford, Connecticut. Hitchcock kept costs low by employing many workers and using inexpensive paper stencils. In the best examples, several stencils were used to create a single design, with freehand embellishments and complex shading enhancing the fruit, flowers, and leaves appearing in endless variety.

A stenciled basket of fruit and golden cornucopias
enrich a circa 1825 maple Baltimore fancy chair (opposite). An unidentified
gentleman (above left) lends his profile to the lyre-shaped center splat
on a cane-seated side chair. Stenciled trees and buildings embellish a fiddleback
chair—named for its violin-shaped splat—from Maine (above right);
the bronzing was added freehand.

While fancy chairs and early Hitchcocks may be out of reach to many of today's collectors, later versions by numerous other makers await the dedicated antiques hunter. Street fairs and country auctions can be a rich source for one-of-a-kind examples decorated by folk artists who viewed the chair as yet another "canvas" for expressing their creativity. Painted furniture is perhaps as popular now as it was in the early 1800s, and many people are decorating their own chairs, rediscovering the age-old crafts of faux painting and stenciling.

A ladder-back side chair (above) sports gold decoration and a cameo landscape on the center splat. A dining room (right) is furnished with painted fancy chairs made around 1815—appropriate furnishings, since the 1836 watercolor by Joseph H. Davis next to the window depicts a couple seated on similar pieces.

HOOKED RUGS

Essentially paintings in fabric, hooked rugs offer vivid, highly personal interpretations of time-honored themes. Farm animals and flowers, stylized geometrics, storybook characters, and even the family dog achieved immortality in the hands of talented "hookers," as makers of these richly colored and textured textiles are known.

Hooked rugs—crafted with fabric strips pulled through a woven background fabric—did not appear in any number until the 1820s, following the introduction of jute burlap. This open-weave material was more suited to a hook than the linen backing of old. To make a rug, thrifty homemakers cut narrow strips from worn-out woolen clothing and used a metal hook—a bent nail would do in a pinch—to draw the strips from the back of the burlap to the front, forming continuous loops on the top surface. The loops were left alone or clipped to form a soft pile.

In the 1850s and 1860s, the ready availability of inexpensive, mass-produced fabrics made hooked rugs more popular than ever. Advertisements for ready-made patterns began appearing in women's magazines such as *Godey's Lady's Book*, and patterns could be purchased from door-to-door salesmen. Like quilting bees, rug-hooking parties and classes became the order of the day.

By the 20th century, cottage industries fostered the large-scale production and distribution of rugs hooked by hand following stenciled patterns. Perhaps the most famous of these commercial operations was founded in the early 1900s by the English missionary and doctor Sir Wilfred T. Grenfell. In Canada's remote areas of

Newfoundland and Labrador, Grenfell promoted rug hooking as way for isolated families to generate income. The rugs, known as "mats," featured polar bears, penguins, and other images of the North, rather than the customary florals, and were sold widely until the 1930s. All are highly sought-after today.

While hooked rugs with original designs are

The owner of a lively rug hooked in 1929 (above) likens its energy to a painting by Vincent van Gogh. The freehand design is one-of-a-kind, unlike another enchanting scene worked on a children's rug (opposite). This porridge-bearing trio was probably hooked from a stenciled pattern in the 1920s or 1930s. Advertisements for designs based on storybook characters such as The Three Bears appeared in women's magazines of the day.

*While collectors tend to favor rugs with animal
themes, floral and geometric designs are also eagerly sought. Rugs
in a variety of sizes and shapes stand out in relief against stark
white walls (above). The smallest piece may have served as
a table or chair pad; both of these forms of hooked textiles are worth
hunting for at tag sales and country auctions.*

preferred by some collectors, those created from commercially sold patterns are no less worthy of attention. Hookers who purchased burlap backing with a design already stenciled on it could still personalize their creations through color choice and individual embellishments. In either case, the best rugs share the same characteristics of any good folk art: naïve perspective, abstract form, graphic images, and effective use of color.

Like all valued collectibles, vintage hooked rugs should be displayed with care, preferably on walls rather than on floors. Rugs may safely be hung either by sewing a long sleeve to the backing and passing a wooden dowel through the sleeve, or by using an artist's canvas stretcher. Rugs hung on a such a frame must first be stitched loosely at intervals to a sturdy fabric such as canvas, which can then be wrapped around the frame and stapled to itself on the backside. Both methods evenly distribute the weight of the textile. Like all older textiles, hooked rugs should be kept away from sunlight.

Hooked rugs include (clockwise from top left) a cottage-industry piece featuring a clever saying; a chicken couple hooked in Maryland in the late 1800s; a Grenfell mat from the Newfoundland and Labrador province; and an early-1900s Dresden Plate design with a bird at each corner.

TABLE RUGS

Pieced-fabric table rugs were a popular 19th-century fashion. Although they were called rugs, these colorful textiles were never intended for the floor but generally used as part of a table centerpiece grouping that might include a vase of flowers or a few artfully arranged books.

Table rugs were stitched and embellished with fanciful designs, usually with floral or geometric shapes embroidered or appliquéd onto a solid background, often in a dark color that set off the motifs to advantage. Some types, called penny rugs, were pieced from circles cut from felt or other cloth using a large 19th-century penny as a template. Others consisted of dozens of hexagons, octagons, rectangles, or diamonds stitched together.

Most table rugs were created at a time when ladies closely followed the crafts columns in popular magazines, stitching decorative covers for everything from teapots to chair seats. Young girls sometimes polished their quilting skills by making these small table pieces, which essentially involved the same needlework techniques as the larger bedcovers. Not all table rugs were made from patterns, however. Creative seamstresses could always improvise with colorful fabric pieces from their scrap baskets; in rural areas, groups such as the Mennonites crafted beautifully bold and graphic examples. The most ornate table rugs tend to be the oldest, while those featuring bold colors and abstract shapes usually date from the 1920s and 1930s.

Appliquéd felt circles and evenly spaced blanket stitches on a
"tongue" border add graphic punch to a New England table rug made around
1900 (opposite). A Native American dough bowl tops an old Mennonite-made table
runner (above), emblazoned with stars made of stuffed work, a type of
padded, three-dimensional appliqué. The brilliant textile provides a burst of
color in this sparely furnished dining room throughout all the seasons.

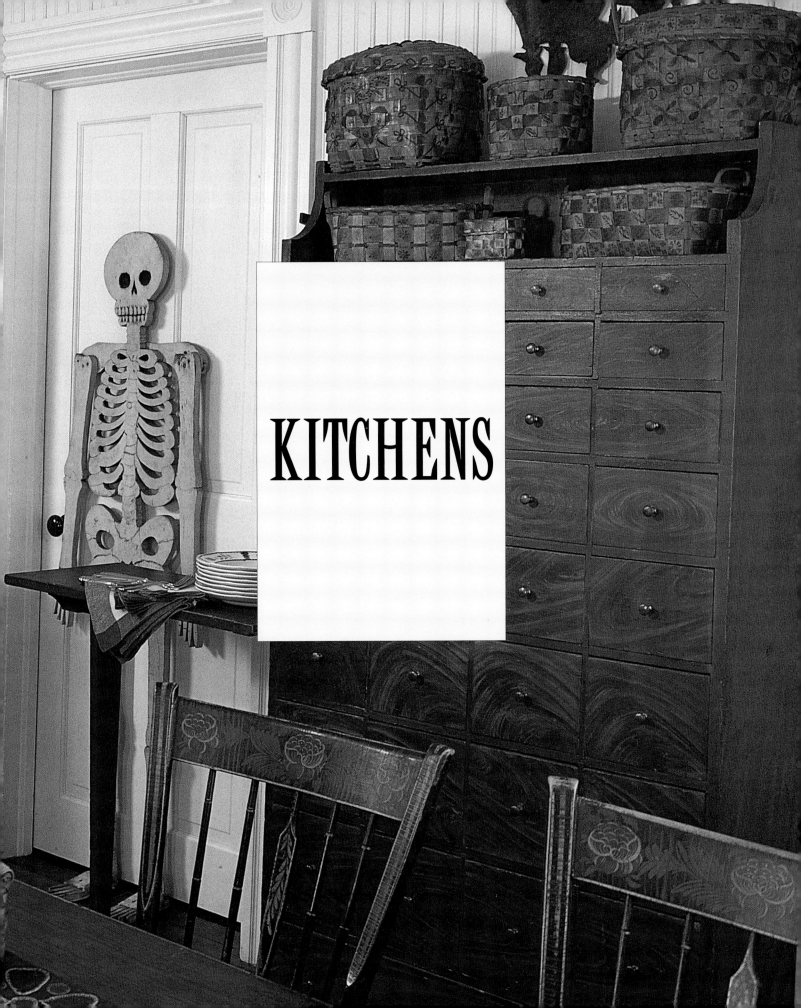

KITCHENS

Until well into the 1800s, cooking routinely took place at the hearth. Coal- and wood-burning ranges began to appear in the 1830s, but several years transpired before these innovative devices caught on. Even when they did, the hearth—which provided the heat and most of the light in the room—remained a symbol of warmth and domesticity.

Despite technological improvements in the generations since, the kitchen is still the heart of the home. Because many families spend a good deal of time in this well-used room, it makes sense to display favorite possessions here. Ceramics, woodenware, and baskets help create a warm atmosphere, introduce welcome color and texture, and provide a foil for the modern look of streamlined kitchen appliances.

It is particularly important to create a good, protected setting for displaying antiques and folk art in the kitchen, where heat and grease are factors. Pieces should be often and carefully dusted, and never placed directly over the stove. Because utensils and kitchen implements are often small, background color is another consideration. A small-print wallpaper, for instance, runs the risk of upstaging a collection; a solid, neutral paint color will always silhouette pieces well and show them off to advantage. (In the past, blue was a common paint color for kitchens, since it was believed to repel flies.) Good lighting will help too. Well-aimed directional lighting is important; recessed bulbs or canister lights fitted onto tracks are also effective. Old pie safes, jelly cupboards, Hoosier cabinets, and other furnishings synonymous with country kitchens are obvious places to house spongeware, mochaware, redware, and many other forms of hand-decorated 19th-century pottery. This is especially true when cupboard doors are fitted with glass or allowed to remain open.

Plate racks also accommodate ceramics to advantage. For collections of colored glass, such as bottles and small vases, glass shelves fitted into a sunny window are a good choice. Even small kitchens have room for a display of baskets, when rafters and ceiling beams are called into service. Wooden utensils such as grain scoops and butter paddles often look their best when suspended from the dowels of a Shaker-style pegboard. If the kitchen is large enough, comfortable, traditional seating such as rocking chairs or an old settle will add to the room's ambiance and encourage friends to linger among the collections while keeping company with the cook.

In a kitchen filled with folk art (overleaf),
Iroquois-made baskets top an unusual paint-decorated apothecary chest,
circa 1810, containing 33 drawers. Dating to the early 1900s,
the skeleton was made for a carnival fun house. New England weather vanes
parade on a bench (above); two field baskets and an antique
cheese basket are tucked underneath.

*An enormous fish and other animals by contemporary craftsman
Stephen Huneck, including a group of sheep—one black—displayed on a grain-painted
table, convene in the sculptor's own Vermont kitchen (above). The newly
built Cape-style house gains architectural interest from antique building elements.
The door came from an old New England town hall, and the fanlight
above the sink was also recycled from a vintage building.*

POTTERY

Until the Revolution, much of the pottery used in America was imported from England. After the war, however, it was not only essential to manufacture goods here but also patriotic duty. Moreover, American clays were plentiful and diverse.

One especially popular folk pottery made in this country was a type of redware coated with slip (a mixture of clay and water blended to the consistency of cream), then incised with a design. Called sgraffito, this centuries-old technique takes its name from the Italian word *sgraffiare*, meaning "to scratch." In this country the decorating method was particularly favored by German settlers in Pennsylvania; the pottery is also known as tulipware after the floral motif much employed in Germanic handcrafts.

Other eye-catching pottery types include spongeware, made with sponged glazing designs applied to a creamware base, and the mottled brown American Rockingham. Lustreware, a delicate-looking pottery made primarily in 19th-century England, was characterized by a metallic finish resembling mother-of-pearl. Mochaware, a type of decorated earthenware, is also especially striking. Made in quantity in the 18th and 19th centuries mainly for taverns, mochaware featured

varied designs, including "cat's eyes," mosslike motifs, and other abstract patterns said to resemble the striations in Arabian mochastone.

Perhaps best-loved of America's folk pottery is salt-glazed stoneware, which originated in Germany's Rhineland region in the 1600s and came to America via England during the same century. This durable and ver-satile pottery was characterized by a hard, pitted surface created when salt was thrown into the kiln during the firing process. Because it was nonporous, the pottery was particularly good for holding liquids, and used for jugs, crocks, pitchers, bottles, and other serviceable vessels that held foodstuffs like cured meats and pickles, along with potables such as beer.

An alcove near an unused side door shelters more than a dozen pieces of salt-glazed stoneware crocks and jugs (opposite). The distinctive decoration was made with a dark metallic oxide known as cobalt blue, favored because it didn't run; a little also went a long way. Mix-and-match stoneware fills the newspaper-trimmed shelves of an old country cupboard (above). A sponge dipped in glaze and dabbed onto the clay created the mottled blue-and-gold decoration on the patterned bowls.

*A lustreware tea set (top) displays the Indian Bonnet pattern and dates
to the 1830s. Popular in 19th-century England, such china was made by both Wedgwood and Spode,
and was prized for its pearl-like finish. A mottled brown glaze distinguishes pieces of American
Rockingham pottery (above), which include a hound-handled pitcher, a cow pitcher, a house bank,
and a lion inkwell. Decorated with cut-sponge and hand-painted patterns, Staffordshire rabbitware
(opposite) was made in England in the 19th century for an American market.*

KITCHENWARE

Using skills and honoring traditions brought from their native lands, European settlers embellished everyday utilitarian items to give as gifts to loved ones as well as for the sheer pleasure of making something more attractive than it needed to be. Indeed, even the humblest household objects made in early America often reflected the impulse to create. Something as basic and practical as a wrought-iron toasting fork, for example, still might be made beautiful with a handle worked into a scroll or heart shape. Similarly, a wooden bowl became a work of art rather than a piece of mundane kitchenware when handcrafted from a piece of wood chosen specifically for its distinctive grain and polished to a deep sheen.

Today early utensils wrought from tin, brass, copper, and iron are displayed with pride in country and city kitchens alike. Early tools for hearth cooking, including waffle irons, trivets, toasting forks, and ladles, stand in their rightful fireside places or form graphic patterns when mounted on walls.

Iron skewers, designed to fix meat and fowl to a roasting spit, often have decorative silhouettes, as do long-handed spatulas and forks, designed to allow the cook to stand back from the fire. Perhaps most coveted of all utilitarian folk art, however, is woodenware, once called treen (from the Anglo-Saxon plural for "tree"). Treen was used for many kinds of kitchen utensils and dishware before pottery works became common after the Revolution. The natural beauty, fine workmanship, and an association with daily life of long ago help account for the popularity of this durable ware, crafted from the many choice species offered by the dense forests of the New World. Hard and sturdy, maple and birch were ideal for mortars and pestles, while the softer varieties of pine might serve for spoons and boxes. Burls—which are large, abnormal growths that appear on the trunks and branches of otherwise healthy trees—were especially prized for their bold, irregular grain (elm, ash, and maple were the most desirable) and made handsome bowls and grain scoops.

Treenware was important: The amount and quality of a household's supply indicated a family's prosperity, or lack of it. In modest circumstances, several family members might share the same wooden plate, or trencher, while in more affluent homes, adults and children each had their own dish.

Wooden boxes were also common household accessories, used to store candles, pipes, and personal documents. Pantry boxes, often constructed in graduated sizes to hold grains, dried fruits, nuts, and other kitchen staples, helped keep order too. Among the most admired of these are Shaker pantry boxes, made by shaping a thin sheet of steamed wood (often maple) around a circular or oval form. Distinctive lapped joints, called fingers, sealed the boxes.

While Shaker boxes are rare—and expensive—

Stacked eight-feet high, these pantry boxes (left) made of pine and painted in jaunty hues make up a rare collection. Collectors often seek boxes in graduated sizes, hoping to amass an impressive assortment such as this. The stack might serve today for storing everything from tools to buttons.

finds, pantry boxes were made widely by many other craftsmen as well, and these can still be found at auctions and in antiques shops. Also worth the hunt are covered buckets called firkins, used to store flour and grains. Like all painted antiques, pieces that wear their original finish are the most valuable.

Other types of collectible woodenware certain to give a kitchen character include rolling pins; those carved from a single piece of wood and small ones made for children are rarest. Maple-sugar molds, and the springerle boards used for making hard cakes and cookies are especially sculptural.

Woodenware gains a rich patina with time, and wear and nicks only contribute to its warmth and appeal. Some experts say old wood has a feel, a sound, and an aroma that an experienced collector can distinguish. Any attempt at cleaning old treen is therefore likely to do more harm than good.

Women as well as men enjoyed working with wood in the 19th century, and both produced boxes for just about every purpose. Knife boxes, or caddies (above), feature a variety of decorative treatments, including grain painting on the box at right on the top shelf. A lidded storage box on the bottom shelf boasts carved designs. A painted pegboard (overleaf) is a good background for woodenware and pottery.

*Chalkware and redware banks (opposite) fill an unusual
steeple-topped shelf found on a farm in the Blue Ridge Mountains
of West Virginia. The stacked document boxes boast their
original finishes. Butter stamps (above) were used to imprint a decorative design
and allowed farm wives to add a personal mark
to identify their butter when it was sold at market.*

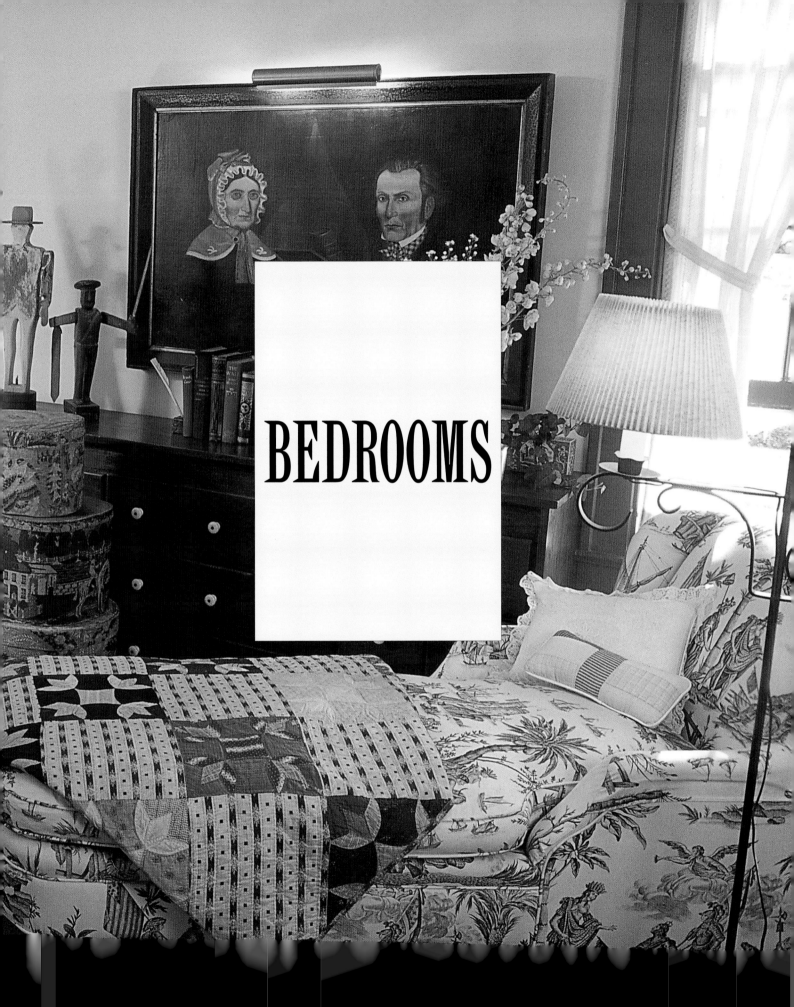

BEDROOMS

While the concept of a separate bedroom is familiar to us now, the idea was not so common in Colonial days. Until the Revolutionary period, it was typical to keep a bed in the all-purpose room known as the "hall," as well as in the parlor, where the finest bed in the household earned a prominent position. Hangings, which provided warmth and privacy, and the coverlets and dust ruffles used to dress the bed were called "furniture," and were valued belongings.

Today the bedroom is a distinctly personal haven, and one that is readily enhanced with folk art. While blanket chests, paint-decorated dressing tables, and bandboxes have a natural home in a bedroom, other folk art treasures, including samplers, portraits, ceramics, and whimsical animal carvings, also earn a rightful place here.

Time-honored textiles find traditional and new uses as well. A single patchwork quilt might warm a bed, while several more are often grouped as striking wall coverings or effectively displayed from the rungs of a stepladder or towel rack. Hooked rugs, too, now appear on walls, where they supply visual interest in much the same way a painting does.

Among the favorite folk art treasures in a collector's bedroom (previous overleaf) are stacked paper-covered bandboxes. A pair of late-19th-century carvings of the angel Gabriel blow their horns over an antique Sheraton bed (opposite). Quilts in blues, greens, and yellows wake up a garret bedroom (above). Layering bedcovers in different styles and patterns works well in such a room, where a cheerful mix of styles reflects the owner's personal touch.

QUILTS

While the idea of sitting for hours at a quilting frame may seem tedious today, in the 18th and 19th centuries such work was considered a relief from the backbreaking housekeeping that filled the lives of most farm wives. Quilting bees afforded social interaction and a respite from the isolation that typified rural life. And, with a needle and thread and a basket of fabric scraps, women found a sorely needed outlet for their creative energies. With brilliant combinations of color and form, quilters captured the spirit of their times and left a legacy that grows more important with each passing year.

Although the art of quilting reached its height in America, it actually originated in medieval Europe—

although no one knows exactly where. The word "quilt" comes from the Latin *culcita*, for "stuffed sack," a fairly accurate description for these textiles, which usually have a layer of warm batting sandwiched between the top and the backing. ("Quilting" refers to the patterned stitching that holds the layers together.) Crafted in England in the 16th and 17th centuries, quilts and the art of making them traveled to America with the first European settlers. Often sewn from worn-out clothing, upholstery, and window curtains, these useful bed covers gained a reputation as an economical means for keeping warm.

The quilts that warmed America's beds—and that captivate collectors today—fall into one of three categories: whole cloth, pieced, and appliquéd. Whole-cloth quilt tops have a uniform ground that is sometimes a single piece of fabric; stitching provides the design. In pieced quilts, fabrics of different colors and patterns are stitched together. Sometimes they are sewn in individual blocks that are later joined. Appliquéd quilts consist of cutout fabric designs applied to a background fabric.

The most elaborate bed coverings, known as "show" quilts, feature spectacular center medallions or

A medley of textiles in bold red, white, and blue enlivens a bedroom (opposite).
Hanging from a dowel, the starred quilt was designed for a crib. The two quilts arrayed on the
rungs of an antique ladder display variations on the Irish Chain pattern. Discovered in
a small antiques shop, an appliquéd butterfly-patterned quilt (above) was most likely stitched in
the 1930s from a kit or a pattern from a magazine. On the wall above it, a Midwestern
Amish quilt displays a characteristically stunning geometric pattern.

imaginative geometric patterns of these essential textiles belie their practicality. With their bold, graphic designs, Amish quilts in particular demonstrate just how beautiful the useful could be.

Amish quilts are recognizable by their geometric patterns worked only in solid-color fabrics. In some Amish textiles, the use of black added high drama to the overall design. Examples produced in Pennsylvania prior to 1940 were almost always sewn from wool, while cotton was the fabric of choice in Ohio and other Midwestern communities.

luxurious fabrics such as chintz and velvet. These include "fancy" quilts, whole-cloth beauties (often all-white) that were elaborately and intricately stitched with quilting, and presentation quilts, made by groups of quilters as a labor of love for a special person or stitched to be sold at auction to raise money for a charitable cause.

More thrifty "utility" quilts, on the other hand, were economically pieced from recycled fabric scraps; everyday quilts, these saw the heaviest use. Often the

Handmade lace borders a mid-19th-century crib quilt (above left),
appliquéd and pieced from polished cotton. The top edge was intentionally left
bare, since it would have been hidden by pillows at the head of the bed.
Mounted on a hinged door, a linen-backed crib quilt cleverly conceals a bedroom
television (above right). The hexagonal mosaic design is one of the early
patchwork patterns used in America, dating to about 1825.

Pattern names furnish intriguing clues to social and religious concerns. Favorite Amish patterns, for instance, included the Star of Bethlehem and were inspired by other religious themes as well. Other names reflected regional folklore or the preferences of the quilter. The Pine Tree design came from the pine tree flag of the Colonies, the Log Cabin and Bear's Paw paid tribute to the pioneer spirit, and the crooked Drunkard's Path illustrated the dreaded outcome of drinking the demon alcohol. Several thousand quilt names have been recorded to date; some patterns are known by more than one name, owing to regional variations.

Considering the hard use and frequent washings quilts often endured, it is no small miracle that many fine examples remain. Their survival indicates how valued the best quilts were. Collectors who still appreciate them today look first at the textile's overall pattern, which should be instantly pleasing, and then at its stitching, which should be fine and even. Condition is also important; holes, stains, and threadbare patches lower the value of a piece considerably. When necessary, valuable quilts should be cleaned and repaired by a professional conservator. Quilts sent to a dry cleaner risk being damaged.

Pattern alone doesn't make a quilt great. Intricate quilting on an appliquéd quilt (above) represents months—even years—of labor. Lively quilting bees helped the work go quickly and provided opportunity for exchanging gossip and news. Quilters gathered around a wooden frame that held the quilt's three layers and prevented them from shifting. A rare Mennonite Zigzag Rainbow quilt dating to the late 19th century covers the guest bed in a summer house (overleaf). Mennonite quilts are generally less conservative than their Amish cousins.

*Often stitched for clergymen and teachers, presentation
quilts such as this Pennsylvania piece (opposite top) bore the signatures of
the friends and colleagues who worked on the individual blocks. A Flower Basket
quilt (opposite bottom) dresses a 19th-century rope bed. Mounted
on a wall, a graphic Tumbling Blocks wool quilt (above) boasts a border
of brocade. The quilt on the bed features appliquéd pinwheels.*

*The Log Cabin pattern is an old favorite and continues
to be pieced today. On this bed (above), a recent version harmonizes to
perfection with antique furnishings. An early-19th-century
Sawtooth quilt (opposite) boasts a border of imported chintz. Quiltmakers
prized the beautiful printed patterns in chintz and often cut out
the individual motifs and used them as appliqués.*

COVERLETS

Like quilts, bed coverlets arrived in America by way of Europe. Woven of linen or wool, those textiles dating from early years of Colonization to the late 1700s were made at home and were the product of a family effort. Men typically cultivated and processed flax, the plant used to make linen, and sheared the sheep raised for wool. Spinning, which yielded linen thread and wool yarn, was typically women's work, while children often helped to card the wool and wind the bobbins.

A good example of Colonial self-sufficiency, coverlet making required few purchased supplies, with the exception of dyes. Sold commercially in concentrated cakes, indigo blue and madder red, which both came from imported plant materials, offered economical alternatives to home-brewed colors. Thus, while the red, white, and blue hues common to so many early American coverlets may appear to be patriotic in nature, they were really born of necessity and practicality.

By the early 1800s, coverlet making had become a male-dominated occupation. At first, itinerant weavers worked in exchange for room and board, using a family's own loom or a community loom. Professionals eventually set up permanent workshops, paying house calls only to pick up wool and to allow a farm wife to choose a design from the weaver's book of patterns.

By 1825, readily available mill-spun thread and the revolutionary new Jacquard loom attachment enabled professional weavers around the country to expand their repertoire considerably. The Jacquard device used a series of punched cards that manipulated the threads into complicated new patterns incorporating circular and other curving shapes never before possible. Not everyone had access to the Jacquard, however, and old standbys, such as the overshot coverlet, continued to be produced as well. Overshots earned their name from a weaving technique that allowed the weft (horizontal) threads to skip, or "overshoot," three or more warp (vertical) threads. The result was a thick but loose-looking weave.

Collectors generally seek out coverlets woven in three or more colors, with such finishing touches as fringe and elaborate borders. Signatures and dates are also desirable. Individual regional touches have their appeal as well; Southern-made coverlets, for example, sometimes feature crooked center seams, thought to drive away evil spirits.

A handwoven coverlet made in an overshot weave dresses an 1840 walnut bed (above). The textile has a well-disguised seam down the middle, indicating it was made on an early, narrow loom; two pieces had to be woven separately, then sewn together. The red-and-blue color scheme indicates the use of indigo blue and madder red, the two commercially sold dyes most readily available to farm wives.

A collection of dated coverlets (above) includes an 1840s
piece displayed on the bed; the pattern of blues and beiges is done in an
overshot weave. Pillows boast circular designs, made possible by
the introduction of the Jacquard loom in the 1820s. Also Jacquard-woven
is a rare three-color coverlet (overleaf). The intricate woven design
is a striking counterpoint to the spare decor.

PAINTED FURNITURE

Polished woods may prevail in today's bedrooms, but in the 18th century, just about all country-made furniture in America was painted, and for good reason. Since several different woods of various hues were often used in a single piece—a Windsor chair, for example, might incorporate maple spindles, a hickory back bow, and a pine seat—a coat of paint was needed to achieve a uniform and pleasing appearance. Paint also provided good protection against insects and moisture, an especially important attribute in early America's poorly insulated houses.

While some paint finishes were intended to camouflage poor-quality wood—making a soft wood look like a more desirable hardwood, for instance—others were applied purely to satisfy the creative urges of a craftsman. In the city, sophisticated artisans practiced "fancy painting" (see pages 98-103). In more isolated rural areas, country furniture makers were equally successful in producing faux finishes that mimicked desirable wood veneers as diverse as cedar, rosewood, bird's-eye and curly maple, birch, walnut, and mahogany.

Sometimes roaming from town to town in search of commissions, country painters learned to take advantage of the least expensive, most readily available materials on hand. Paint recipes made use of pigments

Melons and grapes festoon a 19th-century dressing table (above).
These stenciled fruit motifs were applied over a yellow base coat. This, in turn,
was treated with a grain-painting technique in which strips of putty
were rolled across the surface while it was still wet. Worn edges and heavy
wear around the knobs indicate the dressing table has never
been refinished, adding significantly to its value.

formulated from soot and lampblack, clay, bark, leaves, berries, and animal blood; these were bound with skim and butter milk. (The awful smell of many of these concoctions fortunately dissipated when the paint dried.) Artisans cut stencils from leather, paper, and linen, and found that the long fur of a squirrel's tail could be made into serviceable brushes.

The essential technique for applying a decorative finish to furniture was fairly simple. First, the piece received a base coat that was allowed to dry. A contrasting color followed, which would be manipulated while still wet so that part of the base color would show through to create interesting designs and graining patterns.

A piece of newspaper, a comb, wadded cloth, or even fingertips might be pulled across the surface for a rippled effect. Dabbing with a sponge produced a mottled look, ranging from delicate to bold depending on the absorbency of the sponge. A piece of putty pushed in a circular motion could create the appearance of tortoiseshell. A dried corncob dipped in color, then held firmly at one end and rotated with the other, produced stippled circles. Candle smoke was used to produce dark smudges, and corks were dabbed in paint for intriguing round motifs.

Symbolic images often grace fine examples of painted furniture.
A distinctive worktable from Massachusetts (above), made around 1820, features
a gilt-painted lion and unicorn flanking a central urn; these animals
portend a happy marriage. Each drawer of a veneered bureau (overleaf) boasts
a different scene, showing houses and pastoral views of tree-studded hills.
The style is reminiscent of early-19th-century mural painting.

In addition to grain painting and other decorative imitative finishes, stenciled and freehand designs were also used to embellish beds, cupboards, chairs, chests, tables, and boxes. Often the motifs had symbolic or religious meaning. On the dower chests once given to young women engaged to marry, for example, images might include a tulip with three petals (symbolizing the Holy Trinity), the unicorn (which guarded virginity), a lion (signifying courage), or a peacock (emblem of the Resurrection).

Good examples of painted furniture, once so common, are now difficult to find. All too often, fine pieces were stripped, sanded, and refinished in an attempt to rejuvenate them. Moreover, repainted pieces are frequently passed off as having an original finish, fooling novice collectors into thinking they have discovered something fine. One way to check for this is to examine any nicks, scratches, or cracks. If paint is visible in these telltale areas, it is likely the piece was reworked. Original finishes will also show bare patches on or around wear points, such as the rungs of a chair, or the knobs on a drawer or door.

Two distinctive painted boxes (above) show how effective simple decorative treatments can be. Candle smoke applied over a yellow base coat created the soft, hazy effect on the top piece, while the box beneath it, dated 1847, was grained to look like tortoiseshell. A more recently made piece (opposite) probably dates from the 1940s: the painted motifs reflect the rage for painted furniture started by the original designs of Cape Cod craftsman Peter Hunt, who published popular how-to books.

A three-drawer blanket chest (above), painted to create the effect
of paneling, shows the artistic combination of rag- and comb-graining, tombstone
panels, and borders picked out with stenciled diamond motifs. A bold use
of color and a daring design indicate the piece may hail from Pennsylvania, where
a large number of German immigrants settled in the 18th and 19th centuries.
Many of these were craftsmen who excelled at decorative painting.

Named for the New York county where it was made,
a Schoharie chest (top) is dated 1816. The piece was made with only six boards,
then mounted on a frame with feet. A comb-painted box with little ball feet (above)
may have held a family Bible or documents. A straightforward design and
pure paint colors make a blanket chest from Lancaster County (overleaf) a natural
addition to a bedroom filled with simple Shaker furniture.

GLOSSARY

Apothecary Chest A multi-drawer wooden cabinet used for storing drugs and pharmaceutical compounds; sometimes intricately decorated and cleverly designed with a fold-down table for mixing medicines.

Appliqué A sewing technique in which cut-outs are stitched onto a fabric background; often used for quilts and table rugs.

Bandbox An oval or round container made of thin wood or paperboard and often covered in printed wallpaper; originally used for storing out-of-season clothing.

Braided Rug A floor covering made from long, narrow fabric strips braided together and sewn in a coil (usually round or oval); easiest to make of all rag rugs.

Bulto A religious image of Hispanic origin made in the form of a human figure; usually carved from cottonwood, then covered with gesso and painted.

Butter Mold A device used for imprinting homemade or store-bought tub butter with a decorative motif; usually made of wood with a pattern carved in relief.

Chalkware A type of ornamental object molded from chalky white gypsum (the main ingredient in plaster of Paris). Made for a middle-class market, chalkware was conceived as an inexpensive alternative to Staffordshire.

Coverlet A woven bedspread, usually made from a combination of wool, cotton, and linen; often in the Jacquard or overshot weave.

Crazy Quilt A lap throw or bedcover sewn from randomly shaped fabric pieces; the effect was said to resemble "crazed" porcelain. A crazy quilt is technically not a quilt, since the top and backing are frequently joined by knots rather than decorative stitching, and there is usually no batting.

Creamware A type of hard, lead-glazed pottery with a cream-colored body.

Decoy A carving used by hunters and fishermen to attract water fowl or fish. Life-size bird decoys typically suggest the appearance of ducks, geese, and shore birds. Used in ice fishing, fish decoys mimic the look of various freshwater fish species.

Dower Chest A hand-carved and painted hope chest, sometimes personalized with initials and a date, made for a woman (and infrequently a man) in anticipation of marriage.

Fancy Chair A highly decorated chair made primarily from about the 1820s to the 1850s by skilled craftsmen in East Coast cities. Distinguishing features include faux paint finishes and extensive gilding.

Faux Finish A fool-the-eye paint finish often applied to inexpensive materials in an attempt to imitate the look of those that are more costly, such as mahogany and marble.

Figurehead A decorative carving, often a human or animal figure, positioned under a ship's bowsprit and intended to symbolize the name of the vessel or her guardian spirit.

Firkin A small wooden bucket or cask used for storing kitchen staples.

Fraktur A piece of highly decorative calligraphy, such as a baptismal or wedding certificate, done by Germanic immigrants in the tradition of European illuminated manuscripts.

Grain Painting A decorative painting technique often used on floors and furniture to imitate wood graining; patterns might be worked into the paint with a feather, comb, putty, or even fingertips.

Hitchcock Chair A paint-decorated side chair produced in the Connecticut factory of Lambert Hitchcock (1795-1852).

Hooked Rug A floor covering made from narrow fabric strips, usually of wool, pulled through a fabric backing.

Jacquard Weave A type of weave, used primarily for coverlets, made by using a punch-card loom attachment invented in 1801 by Frenchman Joseph Jacquard and brought to America in the 1820s. The innovative device, which could be used on a standard draw loom, made it possible to weave more quickly and to produce curvilinear motifs.

Kas A generously proportioned wardrobe of Dutch origin, often with bottom drawers, ball feet, and a heavy cornice.

Limner An early term for a portrait painter.

Linsey-Woolsey A coarse, sturdy fabric made of a combination of wool and linen; used by the early Colonists for durable bed covers.

Lustreware A type of decorated pottery distinguished by an iridescent glaze made from metallic oxides.

Lure Artificial bait (usually fish-shaped) fitted with barbs; used on a fishing line for snaring fresh- or saltwater fish.

Mochaware A type of glazed earthenware made to resemble a milky-colored stone known as mocha stone, which is characterized by mosslike markings in green and reddish brown. Mochaware was produced primarily in England from the late 1700s through the 1800s and used extensively in Early American homes and taverns.

Overshot Weave A type of thick, loose weave in which the horizontal (weft) threads were allowed to skip, or overshoot, three or more vertical (warp) threads. Used primarily for coverlets.

Patchwork A sewing technique in which small pieces of cloth in various colors and patterns are sewn together to form a pleasing overall design. Patchwork includes the techniques of piecing and appliqué.

Pendant Pair Two portraits, usually of husband and wife, painted to face each other.

Penny Rug A table cover stitched from circular fabric pieces, usually of felt, cut with a penny-sized template.

Pieced Quilt A quilt with a top made from many small fabric pieces stitched together to form a pleasing pattern.

Quilt A bedcover typically made of three layers—a top, central batting (usually cotton or wool), and a backing—all held together with decorative stitching.

Rag Rug A floor covering made from fabric scraps using one of several techniques, including braiding and hooking.

Redware Simple, inexpensive pottery produced from common brick clay fired to a red color; one of the first pottery types produced in America.

Rockingham A type of yellowware decorated with a distinctive, mottled-brown slip glaze; produced primarily in Vermont, Maryland, and Ohio and popular from about 1850 to 1880.

Rosemaling A decorative paint technique of Norwegian origin noteworthy for its curvilinear forms.

Salt-glazed Stoneware A heavy, durable pottery made from white clay fired at a high temperature. The distinctive pitted glaze was produced by scattering salt into the kiln during the firing process, which created a hard, nonporous surface.

Sampler An embroidered textile, usually made by schoolgirls to demonstrate various kinds of stitches; often includes numerals and letters of the alphabet.

Santo A religious image (such as a saint) of Hispanic origin; may be a painted image or a three-dimensional carving. See Bulto.

Schrank A large wardrobe or linen press often elaborately decorated with painted motifs; brought to America by settlers from the German Palatinate.

Settle A straight-backed bench with arms, and, occasionally, a lift-up seat for storage.

Sgraffito The term used to describe redware decorated with slip and incised designs that expose the red clay base underneath. Sometimes called tulipware.

Silhouette A likeness cut from a solid dark material (usually paper) and mounted on a light background; shows only the outline or general shape of the subject, usually in profile. Name for Etienne de Silhouette, a late 18th-century French controller of finances, perhaps as an allusion to his brief, shadowy tenure.

Slipware Pottery decorated with slip, a thin mixture of colored clay and water, applied with a brush or by dribbling the mixture on the clay surface.

Spongeware Pottery decorated with brightly colored glazes applied with a sponge, often through a stencil, producing a blotchy effect.

Springerle Board An elaborately carved wooden mold for making hard cakes and cookies; used by Germans and other Northern European immigrants.

Sunday Toy A plaything of a religious or educational nature, such as a Noah's ark or a set of alphabet blocks, made expressly for use on Sundays. Also called a Sabbath Day toy.

Table Rug A decorative covering for a table or chest often made with pieced work, appliqué, and embroidery; popular in the Victorian era.

Theorem A painting, usually a still life, produced using a separate stencil for each color; typically worked on paper, canvas, or velvet.

Treen An early term for utilitarian kitchenware made entirely of wood; common in Colonial households in the days before pottery became widely available.

Weather Vane A device, frequently in the shape of an animal or human figure, used for gauging wind direction. Often decorative as well as functional, weather vanes became the quintessential form of American sculpture during the 18th and 19th centuries.

Wedding Anniversary Tin Oversized decorative objects crafted of tin, usually given in jest to couples celebrating their tenth anniversary.

Whirligig A whimsical wind toy, usually part articulated figure and part windmill.

Whole-cloth Quilt A quilted bedcover with a top made with a uniform ground—sometimes a single piece of fabric—and decorated with elaborate stitching.

Windsor Chair A type of chair featuring a spindle back, raking legs, and a saddle seat. The Windsor originated in England as garden furniture and was popular in America during the 18th and 19th centuries.

Yellowware Pottery made with a buff-colored clay base and often decorated with contrasting bands of color.

INDEX

SELECTED BIBLIOGRAPHY

An American Sampler: Folk Art from the Shelburne Museum. National Gallery of Art, 1987.

Andrews, Ruth, editor. *How to Know American Folk Art.* E. P. Dutton & Co., Inc., 1977.

Bishop, Robert. *American Folk Sculpture.* E. P. Dutton & Co., Inc., 1974.

Bishop, Robert, et al. *Folk Art: Paintings, Sculpture & Country Objects.* Alfred A. Knopf, 1983.

Bishop, Robert. *Quilts, Coverlets, Rugs & Samplers.* Alfred A. Knopf, Inc., 1982.

Bossert, Helmuth. *Folk Art of Europe.* Rizzoli International, 1990.

Brackman, Barbara. *Clues in the Calico: A Guide to Identifying and Dating Antique Quilts.* EPM Publications, Inc., 1989.

Fales, Dean A., Jr. *American Painted Furniture 1660-1880.* E. P. Dutton, 1979.

Garrett, Elisabeth Donaghy. *At Home: The American Family 1750-1870.* Harry N. Abrams, Inc., 1990.

Granick, Eve Wheatcraft. *The Amish Quilt.* Good Books, 1989.

Hall, Dinah. *Ethnic Interiors.* Rizzoli International, 1992.

Kent, Kate Peck. *Navajo Weaving: Three Centuries of Change.* School of American Research Press, 1985.

Ketchum, William C., Jr. *American Redware.* Henry Holt, 1991.

Kopp, Joel and Kate. *American Hooked and Sewn Rugs: Folk Art Underfoot.* E. P. Dutton & Co., Inc., 1975.

Lipman, Jean, and Alice Winchester. *The Flowering of American Folk Art.* The Viking Press, Inc., 1974.

Lipman, Jean, et al. *Young America: A Folk Art History.* Hudson Hills Press, 1986.

Lipman, Jean, et al. *Five-Star Folk Art: One Hundred American Masterpieces.* Harry N. Abrams, Inc., in association with The Museum of American Folk Art, 1990.

Little, Nina Fletcher. *Country Arts in Early American Homes.* E. P. Dutton & Co., Inc., 1975.

Mackey, William F., Jr. *American Bird Decoys.* Schiffer Publishing Ltd., 1965.

Miller, Margaret M., and Sigmund Aarseth. *Norwegian Rosemaling.* Charles Scribner's Sons, 1974.

Orlofsky, Patsy and Myron. *Quilts in America.* Abbeville Press, 1992.

Reno, Dawn E. *American Indian Collectibles.* The House of Collectibles, 1988.

Rumford, Beatrix T., and Carolyn J. *Treasures of American Folk Art from the Abby Aldrich Rockefeller Folk Art Center.* Little, Brown and Company, in association with the Colonial Williamsburg Foundation, 1989.

Schaffner, Cynthia V. A. *Discovering American Folk Art.* Harry N. Abrams, Inc., 1991.

Sprigg, June. *Shaker Design.* Whitney Museum of American Art in association with W. W. Norton & Co., 1986.

Stewart, Regina, and Geraldone Cosentino. *Stoneware.* Golden Press, 1977.

Warren, Elizabeth V., and Stacy C. Hollander. *Expressions of a New Spirit: Highlights from the Permanent Collection of the Museum of American Folk Art.* Museum of American Folk Art, 1989.

PHOTOGRAPHY CREDITS

1, 2 Keith Scott Morton, 4-5 Keith Scott Morton, 6 Jessie Walker, 8 Keith Scott Morton, 10, 12 Jessie Walker, 13 Arthur Griggs, 14 Paul Kopelow (left) Arthur Griggs (right), 15 Arthur Griggs (left) Allan Baillie (right), 16, 17, 18 Jessie Walker, 18-19 Jessie Walker, 20 (top and bottom), 21 Keith Scott Morton, 22 Paul Kopelow (left) Keith Scott Morton (right), 23 Paul Kopelow (left) Jessie Walker (right), 24-25 Keith Scott Morton, 26 Paul Kopelow (left) Jon Elliot (right), 27 Jon Elliot (left and right), 28 Keith Scott Morton, 29 Jessie Walker, 30-31 Keith Scott Morton, 32 (left and right), 33 Keith Scott Morton, 34 Philip Thompson, 35, 36 Keith Scott Morton, 37 William Stites, 38 Paul Nystrom, 39 Paul Kopelow, 40-41 Keith Scott Morton, 42 Michael Dunne, 43 Keith Scott Morton, 44 Rick Patrek, 45 Keith Scott Morton, 46-47 Al Teufen, 48, 49 Keith Scott Morton, 50 Jessie Walker, 51 Paul Kopelow, 52-53 Keith Scott Morton, 54 Keith Scott Morton, 54 Paul Kopelow, 55 Jessie Walker, 56-57 Charles Nesbit, 58 Keith Scott Morton (top) Paul Kopelow (bottom), 59, 60 Jessie Walker, 61 Charles Nesbit, 62 Paul Kopelow, 62-63 Keith Scott Morton, 64 Paul Kopelow, 65 Keith Scott Morton, 66 Jessie Walker, 67 Jessie Walker (left) Paul Kopelow (right), 68-69 James Levin, 70 Jessie Walker, 71 Keith Scott Morton (top) Paul Kopelow (bottom), 72-73 Keith Scott Morton, 74 Paul Kopelow, 75 Keith Scott Morton, 76 Jessie Walker, 77 (left and right), 78 Keith Scott Morton, 79 Joshua Greene, 80 Lynn Karlin, 80-81 Keith Scott Morton, 82 Paul Kopelow (left and right), 83 Jessie Walker (left) Paul Kopelow (right), 84-85 Keith Scott Morton, 86-87 Keith Scott Morton, 88, 89 Keith Scott Morton, 90 Paul Kopelow, 91 Keith Scott Morton, 92-93 Keith Scott Morton, 92-93 James Levin, 94 Paul Kopelow, 95 Al Teufen, 96 Paul Kopelow, 97 Keith Scott Morton, 98 Keith Scott Morton (left) James Levin (right), 99 James Levin, 100 Keith Scott Morton, 101 James Levin (left and right), 102 James Levin, 102-103 Keith Scott Morton, 104 Paul Kopelow, 105 Jessie Walker, 106 Keith Scott Morton, 107 Paul Kopelow (top left) Keith Scott Morton (top right) Keith Scott Morton (center) Paul Kopelow (bottom), 108 Paul Kopelow, 109 Keith Scott Morton, 110-111 Keith Scott Morton, 112 Jessie Walker, 113 Keith Scott Morton, 114 Paul Kopelow, 115 Jessie Walker, 116 Keith Scott Morton (top) Jessie Walker (bottom), 117 Jessie Walker, 118 Paul Kopelow, 119 Keith Scott Morton, 120-121 Paul Kopelow, 122, 123 Jessie Walker, 124-125 Keith Scott Morton, 126 Keith Scott Morton, 127 Ralph Bogertman, 128 Jessie Walker, 129, 130 Keith Scott Morton (left and right), 131 Jessie Walker, 132-133 Keith Scott Morton, 134 Charles Nesbit (top) Keith Scott Morton (bottom), 135 Keith Scott Morton, 136 Paul Kopelow, 137 Keith Scott Morton, 138 Al Teufen, 139 Keith Scott Morton, 140-141 Jessie Walker, 142, 143 James Levin, 144-145 James Levin, 146 James Levin, 147 Jessie Walker, 148, 149 Paul Kopelow (top and bottom), 150-151 Jon Elliot, 152 Paul Kopelow, 156, 160 Keith Scott Morton.